Student Study
Cliff Roberson, LLM, rii.u.
Washburn University

Criminal Law Today
An Introduction with Capstone Cases
THIRD EDITION

Frank Schmalleger, Ph.D.
Professor Emeritus
The University of North Carolina at Pembroke

PEARSON
Prentice Hall

Upper Saddle River, New Jersey 07458

Executive Editor: Frank Mortimer, Jr.
Assistant Editor: Sarah Holle
Exectutive Marketing Manager: Tim Peyton
Managing Editor: Mary Carnis
Production Editor: Barbara Marttine Cappuccio
Director of Manufacturing and Production: Bruce Johnson
Manufacturing Manager: Ilene Sanford
Manufacturing Buyer: Cathleen Petersen
Senior Design Coordinator: Mary E. Siener
Cover Design: Vicki Kane
Cover Image: GettyImages/Corbis
Printing and Binding: Command Web

Pearson Prentice Hall™ is a trademark of Pearson Education, Inc.
Pearson® is a registered trademark of Pearson plc
Prentice Hall® is a registered trademark of Pearson Education, Inc.

Pearson Education LTD.
Pearson Education Singapore, Pte. Ltd
Pearson Education, Canada, Ltd
Pearson Education–Japan
Pearson Education Australia PTY, Limited
Pearson Education North Asia Ltd
Pearson Educación de Mexico, S.A. de C.V.
Pearson Education Malaysia, Pte. Ltd

10 9 8 7 6 5 4 3 2 1
ISBN 0-13-170291-2

Contents

	Introduction	v
Chapter 1	The Nature and History of Criminal Law	1
Chapter 2	Criminal Liability and the Essence of Crime	13
Chapter 3	Expanding the Concept of Crime	24
Chapter 4	Extending Criminal Liability: Inchoate Offenses and Parties to Crime	31
Chapter 5	Justifications as Defenses	44
Chapter 6	Excuses as Defenses	53
Chapter 7	The Defense of Insanity	62
Chapter 8	Legal and Social Dimensions of Personal Crime: Homicide	70
Chapter 9	Legal and Social Dimensions of Personal Crime: Assault, Battery, and Other Personal Crimes	81
Chapter 10	Legal and Social Dimensions of Property and Computer Crimes	93
Chapter 11	Offenses Against Public Order and the Administration of Justice	106
Chapter 12	Offenses Against Public Morality	118
Chapter 13	Victims and the Law	128
Chapter 14	Punishment and Sentencing	138

Introduction

This Study Guide was created to be a supplemental learning tool to Frank Schmalleger's *Criminal Law Today: An Introduction with Capstone Cases*, 3rd ed. Before using this Study Guide, you should read the chapters of the textbook carefully. This guide is designed to assist you in learning the criminal law principles and concepts discussed in the textbook. The chapters of the study guide correspond directly to the chapters of the textbook. To understand criminal law, you need to "attack it" from several approaches. First, study the chapter in the text, then read the notes in this study guide, and finally complete the study questions and review exercises for each chapter. The study guide chapters are divided into six sections, as follows:

1. *Chapter Summary*. The summaries are designed to provide you with an overview of the general principles and concepts in each chapter.

2. *Capstone Cases*: *Learning Issues*. Learning issues are included in the chapters to assist you in understanding the capstone cases and recognizing the significant issues in those cases.

3. *Practice Test Questions*. These questions were created to test your comprehension of the materials presented in the textbook. There are multiple choice and true-false questions in each chapter.

4. *Key Concepts*. This is a definitional exercise involving the key concepts set forth in the chapter.

5. *Factual Scenarios*. The factual scenarios were created to help you put the reading material into a broader perspective, and generate discussion about important criminal law principles and concepts.

6. *Crossword Puzzles*. Included in each chapter is a crossword puzzle. The crossword puzzle numbers also correspond directly to the chapters in the text.

If you have any questions or have suggestions on how to improve this study guide, Dr. Schmalleger can be contacted at www.cjtoday@adelphia.net.

Sincerely,

Cliff Roberson, LLM, Ph.D.
Washburn University

Chapter 1

The Nature and History of Criminal Law

CHAPTER SUMMARY

I. Introduction

In the example given in this section of the text, the offender was charged with taking a vehicle without the owner's permission, a misdemeanor punishable by less than a year in jail. Under the facts set forth in the text, the offender could probably have been charged with automobile theft, which in most states is a felony.

II. What Is Criminal Law?

The problems and issues involved in deciding what behavior should be criminal are complex. Consider the difference between social norms that do not violate the law and social norms which constitute violations of criminal law. Why are some norms and mores enforced by the use of criminal law concepts and others are not? Distinguish between behavior that is merely deviant behavior and behavior that is both deviant and criminal. What types of deviant behavior may properly be called "criminal?"

You should understand the problems involved in defining the terms "crime" and "criminal laws." Sutherland's definition of crime as that behavior which is prohibited by the State as an injury to the State and against which the State may react provides a good starting point for defining crime.

Criminal law can be understood as that body of rules and regulations which defines and specifies punishments for offenses of a public nature, or for wrongs committed against the state or society. Criminal law is also called penal law.

A. Types of Crime

There are four basic types of crimes: treason, felonies, misdemeanors, and infractions. The distinguishing feature between the types of crimes is the degree of punishment that may be imposed upon conviction of each type. Treason and felonies are considered as the serious crimes. Treason is a relatively rare crime. Felonies are generally punishable by incarceration in a prison or correctional institution for a period in excess of one year. Misdemeanors are generally punishable by less than a year's incarceration in a jail.

Crimes are also classified as either completed crimes or those which are attempted or still in the planning stage. Inchoate refers to those partial or unfinished crimes. They are discussed in Chapter 4.

Crimes are either *mala in se* or *mala prohibita*. *Mala in se* crimes are those crimes that are traditionally regarding as wrong in themselves. *Mala prohibita* are considered as wrong only because they are prohibited by law. Murder would be a mala in se crime whereas driving 60 MPH in a 55 MPH zone would be a mala prohibita crime.

Crimes are also traditionally divided into four types: property, personal, public order, and morals. Property offenses include theft, forgery, arson, bad checks, and burglary. Personal crimes include rape, criminal homicide, kidnapping, and assault and battery. Public order offenses are also referred to as crimes against the public order and include fighting, breach of peace, disorderly conduct, vagrancy, loitering, and public intoxication.

B. Types of Law

Law, like crime, may be divided into types. Substantive law refers to that part of the law which creates and defines fundamental rights and duties. Substantive criminal law defines crimes and specifies punishments. Procedural law specifies the methods to be used in enforcing substantive law. Substantive law is that which declares what acts are crimes and describes the punishment thereof, whereas procedural law is that which provides or regulates the steps by which one who has violated a criminal statute is punished.

Case law is sometimes referred to as "judge-made" law. It refers to the body of previous decisions, or precedents, which have accumulated over time and to which attorneys refer when arguing cases, and to which judges use in deciding the merits of new cases. Statutory law is law that was created by statutes or formal written strictures and is made by a legislature or governing body with the power to make law. Case law and statutory law make for predictability in the law.

Criminal law was defined earlier. It must be distinguished from civil law. Civil law governs relationships between parties. It regulates contracts, inheritances, and adoptions. A private or civil wrong is a tort. A tort is an unlawful violation of a private right other than a mere breach of contract. Only a criminal law may provide for criminal punishments.

III. The Purpose of Law

Max Weber states that the primary purpose of law is to regulate the flow of human interaction. Without laws of some sort modern society probably could not exist, and social organization would be unable to rise above the level found in primitive societies. Laws also make for predictability in human events by using the authority of the government to ensure that certain standards of behavior will be followed, and enforced. Laws provide a stable foundation for individuals to join together in a legitimate undertaking by enforcing rights over the control and ownership of property.

To many people, a society without laws is unthinkable. If such a society existed, would it be ruled by powerful groups and individuals? The personal whims of the powerful would rule, and those without power would live in constant fear of attack.

A. Moral Enterprise

Should law be used as a tool for social engineering? Study Roscoe Pound's postulates which he contends form the basis of all law because they reflect shared needs. Note that Pound modified them to reflect that laws cannot equally meet the interests of all social groups in any particular society. Understand the role of public interest groups in passing Megan's law and three-strikes legislation.

Howard Becker used the term **moral entrepreneurs** to refer to those who work to enact desired legislation. As Becker noted: "Rules are made automatically."

B. The Role of Criminal Law

Criminal law is a formal social control mechanism. Some contend that the purpose of criminal law is to make society safe for its members, and to punish and rehabilitate those who commit offenses. The text contains a list of criminal law functions on page 12. Review the list. Should any more functions be added to the list? Any deleted?

C. The Rule of Law

Study the concepts involved in "the rule of law." The rule of law has been called the greatest political achievement of our culture. Review the American Bar Association's definition of it. Why do some people refer to the rule of law as the greatest political achievement of our culture?

The rule of law includes the notion that due process of law, or those procedures which effectively guarantee individual rights in the face of criminal prosecution, may be defined as the due course of legal proceedings according to the rules and forms which have been established for the protection of individual rights. Due process means that laws may not be created or enforced in arbitrary or unreasonable fashion. The fifth and fourteenth amendments to the U.S. Constitution provide for due process rights.

IV. Historical Sources of Today's Law

Our criminal laws are shaped by a number of historical antecedents and philosophical perspectives. Important roots include natural law, the Old and New Testaments, religious beliefs and practices, early Roman law, and English common law.

A. Natural Law

Natural law adherents claim that some laws are fundamental to human nature and are discoverable by human reason, intuition, or inspiration, without the need for reference to man-made laws. The concept of "natural law" was used in the philosophical speculations of Roman jurists. It was intended to denote a system of rules and principles for the guidance of human conduct which, independent of enacted law or systems peculiar to any one people, might be discovered by the rational intelligence of man, and would be found to grow out of and conform to his "nature." "His nature" refers to his whole mental, moral, and physical constitution.

Natural law advocates contend that man-made laws should conform to principles inherent in natural law. Consider the concept of natural law and how it affects the abortion issue.

B. Early Codes

The development of criminal codes can be traced to the Code of Hammurabi. This code was named after the Babylonian King Hammurabi and it specified a number of property rights and crimes and associated punishments. Roman law appears to have influenced our own legal tradition in many ways. Roman law was codified under the Emperor Justinian I. The Justinian Code consisted of three legal documents: (1) the Institutes, (2) the Digest, and (3) the Code itself. When Emperor Claudius conquered England in the mid-first century and Roman authority over "Britannia" was consolidated by later rulers, Roman customs, law, and language were forced upon the English population.

C. Common Law

When William the Conqueror invaded England in 1066, he declared the Saxon law absolute. William, seeking to add uniformity to the law, ordered judicial decisions be recorded and disseminated. The enumeration of the various kinds of offenses for which punishment could be meted out led to the concept of "common law crimes." Eventually, common law arose out of prevailing customs, rules, and social practices that found support in an ever-evolving body of judicial decisions. Common law was the result of precedent and tradition. Its authority rested primarily upon usage and custom rather than upon any official degree or statutory enactment.

A few states have passed legislation officially institutionalizing common law principles. In other states, common law principles and precedent of common law continue to hold sway. Even in code jurisdictions, the principles and strictures of common law are generally reflected in statutes.

D. U.S. Constitution

The U.S. Constitution is our "supreme law of the land." The constitution and its amendments provide an important source of today's laws. The constitution acts more as restraints on the authority of the government and protector of our individual rights.

V. The Federal System

Our federal system of government is one in which two governments, federal and state, have jurisdiction over the inhabitants. Each body has control over activities that occur within its legal sphere of influence.

VI. The Model Penal Code

The Model Penal Code is not law, but is a proposed model which states may use as a guide for developing or revising their statutory codes. It was first published by the American Law Institute in 1962. Since that time, it has been revised 13 times.

It is an important document because it attempts to achieve standardization in American criminal law and has served as a model for many state statutes. It also contains legal formulations created by some of the most cogent thinkers in American jurisprudence.

Capstone Case: Learning Issues

Payne v. Tennessee:
   In two earlier cases, *Booth* and *Gathers*, the Supreme Court had held that the Eighth Amendment prohibits a jury from considering a victim impact statement at the sentencing phase of a capital trial.

1. What does the Court mean by a "capital trial?"
2. What constitutes a "victim impact statement?"
3. What does the Eight Amendment prohibit?
4. The Court stated that it granted certiorari (petition for review) to reconsider its holding. Why would the court do that?
5. The Court noted that the consideration of the harm caused by the crime has been an important factor used by trial judges in determining the appropriate sentence. How much weight should a judge place on this factor? Should the harm caused by the crime be considered in those cases where the defendant intended to commit murder, but because of his or her lack of ability fired a weapon at the victim and missed, therefore causing no harm to the victim? The defendant's motive and intent were the same as in a case where the victim was killed.
6. What does the Court mean when it stated that "Eighth Amendment erects no per se bar" if a State chooses to permit the admission of victim impact evidence?

PRACTICE TEST QUESTIONS

MULTIPLE CHOICE

____ 1.1.   When looking at rules of conduct, philosophers talk of morals and morality, whereas sociologists distinguish between

a. morals and morality.
b. norms and mores.
c. law and ethics.
d. ethics and mores.

___ 1.2.   Anyone who intentionally violates a social norm may be considered as
a. inadequately socialized.
b. a criminal.
c. inadequately socialized and a criminal.
d. violating a legally binding rule of society.

___ 1.3.   A(n) ____ is a rule that govern serious violations of the social code.
a. norm
b. more
c. law
d. crime

___ 1.4.   Any act or omission prohibited by public law, committed without defense or justification, and made punishable by the state in a judicial proceeding in its own name is a(n)
a. more.
b. norm.
c. taboo and a tort.
d. crime.

___ 1.5.   A ____ crime is a crime that is said to be inherently evil and immoral.
a. *mala in se*
b. *mala prohibita*
c. *malum prohibit*
d. felony

___ 1.6.   Public order offenses include
a. bad checks.
b. motor vehicle thefts.
c. vandalism.
d. public intoxication.

___ 1.7.   Clarence Ray Jeffery would define "natural crime" as a crime against
a. society.
b. the state.
c. the laws of nature.
d. Congress.

_____ 1.8.   A crime punishable by imprisonment in a state prison is a(n)
               a. *mala in se.*
               b. misdemeanor.
               c. infraction.
               d. felony.

_____ 1-9.   A law which defines crime is a
               a. substantive criminal law.
               b. procedural law.
               c. tort law.
               d. law of punishments.

_____ 1.10.   A law which establishes the punishment for a crime is a
               a. substantive criminal law.
               b. procedural law.
               c. tort law.
               d. law of punishments.

_____ 1.11.   A law which specifies the methods to be used in the trial of a case is a
               a. substantive law.
               b. procedural law.
               c. tort law.
               d. law of punishments.

_____ 1.12.   Case law is often referred to as
               a. code law.
               b. statutory law.
               c. procedural law.
               d. judge-made law.

_____ 1.13.   A violation of a private legal right is a(n)
               a. tort.
               b. infraction.
               c. crime.
               d. violation of a public duty.

_____ 1.14.   A _____ is more concerned with assessing liability than intent.
               a. civil law
               b. public law
               c. private law
               d. regulatory statute

_____ 1.15.   The term _____ refers to the activities of moral crusaders through which new laws
               are created.
               a. moral enterprise.

b. moral leaders.
c. moral advocates.
d. moral crisis.

___ 1.16. The laws that require public notification whenever previously convicted sex offenders move into the neighborhood are called ____ laws.
a. three strikes
b. Megan's
c. open book
d. freedom of information

___ 1.17. The "rule of law" is often referred to as
a. the constitution.
b. case law.
c. the supremacy of law.
d. *stare decisis.*

___ 1.18. Common law was the result of ____ and tradition.
a. legislation
b. the church
c. the king
d. precedent

___ 1.19. Those states that have enacted legislation to the effect that no conduct constitutes an offense unless it is a crime or violation under a specific statute are called
a. common law states.
b. code jurisdictions.
c. due process states.
d. equity states.

___ 1.20. The ____ is not a law, but a proposed model which states may use in developing or revising their criminal codes.
a. American Law Institute Plan
b. Code of England
c. Code of Criminal Law and Procedure
d. Model Penal Code

TRUE/FALSE

___ 1.21. Social norms can often be violated with relative impunity.

___ 1.22. Bigamy is a morals offense.

___ 1.23. Case law is sometimes referred to as statute-made law.

____ 1.24.   *Mala in se* literally means "standing by decided matters."

____ 1.25.   Case law and statutory law make for predictability in law.

____ 1.26.   Civil law governs relationships between individuals and the state.

____ 1.27.   Max Weber contended that the primary purpose of law is to regulate the flow of human interaction.

____ 1.28.   The Justinian Code contained only public laws.

____ 1.29.   The controlling element in common law is precedent.

____ 1.30.   The *Commentaries on the Laws of England* were written by Roscoe Pound.

KEY CONCEPTS

Identify the below key concepts from Chapter 1 of the text:

_____ 1.1.   Unwritten rules that underlie and are inherent in the fabric of society.

_____ 1.2.   A serious crime, generally one punishable by death or incarceration in a prison facility.

_____ 1.3.   The law in the form of statutes or formal written codes, made by a legislature or governing body with the power to make law.

_____ 1.4.   That aspect of the law that specifies the methods to be used in enforcing substantive law.

_____ 1.5.   A private or civil wrong or injury.

_____ 1.6.   The form of law that governs the relationships between parties.

_____ 1.7.   An individual who commits a tort.

_____ 1.8.   The philosophy of law; the science and study of law.

_____ 1.9.   The maxim that an orderly society must be governed by established principles and known codes that are applied uniformly and fairly to all of its members.

_____ 1.10.   Rules of conduct inherent in human nature and in the natural order, which are thought to be knowable through intuition, inspiration, and the exercise of reason without the need for reference to man-made laws.

_____ 1.11.　　Law originating from use and custom rather than from written statutes.

_____ 1.12.　　Those states that have enacted legislation recognizing as criminal only that conduct specifically prohibited by statute.

_____ 1.13.　　Jurisdictions in which the principles and precedents of common law continue to hold sway.

_____ 1.14.　　The authority of a state to enact and enforce a criminal statute.

_____ 1.15.　　To declare an act or omission to be criminal or in violation of a law making it so.

_____ 1.16.　　The authority of a court to hear and decide an action or lawsuit.

_____ 1.17.　　A model code of criminal laws intended to standardize general provisions of criminal liability, sentencing, defenses, and the definitions of specific crimes between and among the states.

_____ 1.18.　　Acts that are considered as "wrongs" only because there are laws against them.

_____ 1.19.　　A violation of a local ordinance that is punishable only by a fine.

_____ 1.20.　　That part of the law that defines crimes and specifies punishments.

FACTUAL SCENARIOS

1. Dr. Hamel was walking on the beach in North Carolina. He saw an individual who was bleeding. Dr. Hamel could easily have stopped the bleeding and saved his life. But he did not want to get involved so he continued his walking. Did Dr. Hamel commit a criminal act? Did he commit an act that was morally wrong? Would it make a difference if the bleeding person was Dr. Hamel's 12-year-old stepson?

2. Jerry White wants to be an attorney. He has a criminal conviction for failure to register for the Selective Service draft, a felony. The State Bar Rules disqualify anyone who has been convicted of a _mala in se_ crime. Should this disqualify him from being an attorney? Would your answer be any different if he was convicted of a petty theft, a misdemeanor?

3. Connie is raped in a local motel. The offender is prosecuted and convicted of forcible rape. Connie now wants to sue the rapist and the motel operator in civil court. What type of action would she bring?

4. Frank, a rich Texan, loves to hunt. He does not like to pay taxes and fees. He is arrested for hunting without a license and given jail time of 30 days, the maximum sentence for that offense. What type of crime has he committed?

5. Robert was convicted of murdering a three-year-old boy. At the sentencing phrase of his trial the prosecution wishes to present evidence that as a direct result of the murder, the victim's mother committed suicide. As judge would you allow this evidence to be admitted? Should the judge allow the defense to enter evidence that the victim's mother attempted to sell her son to another couple shortly before the murder?

CROSSWORD 1

Across

1. A serious crime
5. A civil wrong
9. The authority of a court to hear a case
11. An individual charged with a crime
12. Jurisdictions in which the principles and precedents of common law continue to hold sway are called ___ law jurisdictions.
15. States that have enacted legislation recognizing as criminal only that conduct specifically prohibited by statute are called ___ jurisdictions.
16. A crime discussed in U.S Constitution
18. A public offense
20. A supreme court justice
22. An individual who represents the state in a criminal trial
23. A legislative enactment
24. A law that governs relationships between parties
25. Arson and theft are ___ crimes.

Down

2. An issue in the confirmation hearings on Justice Thomas was ___ law.
3. That body of law and regulations that govern the trial of a case
4. Penal law is also called ___ law.
6. That body of law that defines crimes and establishes punishments
7. A crime punishable by a jail sentence
8. A minor offense
10. The party being sued in a civil case
12. The body of previous decisions is called ____ law.
13. Unwritten rules that underlie and are inherent in the fabric of society
14. ___ crimes are also considered as violent crimes.
17. Legislative enactments are called ___ law.
19. Ethical principles
21. Unwritten, but generally known, rules that govern serious violations of the social code

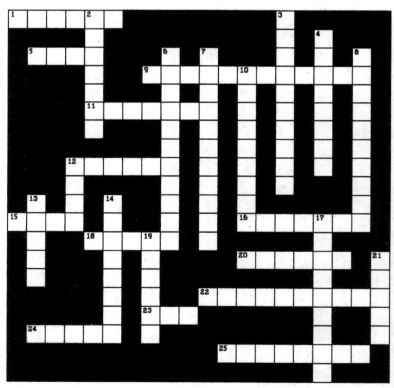

Chapter 2
Criminal Liability and the Essence of Crime

CHAPTER SUMMARY

I. Introduction

A defendant is presumed innocent until the government proves contrary and the government has the burden of proving every essential element beyond a reasonable doubt before the accused may be legally convicted of a crime. The purpose of the Court's instructions to a jury is to provide the jury with the correct principles of law to apply the facts and determine if the defendant's guilt has been proven beyond a reasonable doubt.

II. The Adversarial System

Our system is an adversarial system with the judge acting as the referee. The advocacy model is built upon the premise that truth is the ultimate goal of any criminal trial and that truth can best be realized through effective debate over the merits of opposing perspectives. The adversarial system requires that advocates for both sides do their utmost within boundaries set by law. To guide the behavior of the attorneys, the American Bar Association has created a number of ethical codes. In addition, each state has adopted codes of professional responsibility. Attorneys must adhere to the state codes or risk discipline.

A. Standards of Proof

Look at Judge Ito's instruction to the jury that: "The prosecution has the burden of proving beyond a reasonable doubt each element of the crimes charged in the information and that the defendant was the perpetrator of any such charged crimes." The defendant is not required to prove himself or herself innocent or to prove that any other person committed the crimes charged. The burden is on the prosecution to prove the defendant's guilt.

The reasonable doubt standard plays a vital role in the scheme of criminal procedure. The standard is intertwined with the burden of proof requirement. The burden of proof requirement is an obligation imposed on the prosecution and the standard of proof is a criterion by which this burden must be met if a conviction is to be obtained.

The Supreme Court has never precisely defined "reasonable doubt." It has been defined as follows: It is an actual and substantial doubt arising from the evidence, from the facts or circumstances shown by the evidence, or from the lack of evidence. Contrast that standard with the lesser standard of preponderance of the evidence that is required in a civil case. Also note that between those two standards is the "clear and convincing" standard.

B. Criminal Liability

The term criminal liability can be used to describe the degree of blameworthiness assigned to the defendant after processing by a court, and the concomitant extent to which the defendant is subject to penalties prescribed by the criminal law. The primary purpose of any criminal trial is the determination of the defendant's degree of criminal liability, if any. The degree of criminal liability equals violation of the criminal law minus defenses or justifications.

Understand the distinction between legal guilt and factual guilt. Factual guilt deals with the issues of whether or not the defendant is actually responsible for the crime. Legal guilt is established only when the defendant has been found guilty by a court.

III. The Legal Essence of Criminal Conduct

All crimes share certain features or elements. All crimes can be said to have certain general elements in one form or another. The essence of crime consists of three conjoined and essential elements: the criminal act, a culpable mental state, and the concurrence of the two.

Some would add the concept of harm or a harmful result to the list of elements that constitute the essence of crime. Conduct, as used in the text, encompasses both behavior and one's mental state that was present at the time of the behavior.

A. The Criminal Act

A person must commit some act before he or she is subject to criminal sanctions. Such act is the *actus reus* of the crime. Thinking is not doing. Generally we are not punished for our thoughts. Being and doing are two different things. To be something is not a crime. It is not a crime to be addicted to drugs. It is a crime to use illegal drugs. Generally, the criminal law requires that a person's actions must be voluntary for them to carry criminal liability.

Possession is generally considered a voluntary form of action if the possessor knowingly obtains or receives the thing possessed or is aware of his or her control of the thing for a sufficient time to permit him or her to terminate control. The distinction between knowing possession and mere possession is critical in many cases. Constructive possession means that, at a given time, a person may not have actual physical custody, but is still able to control or influence it.

Failure to act may be criminal under certain situations. Generally, failure to act is a crime only in those situations where the person is required by law to do something or where the law specifies a duty to act. Threatening to act can be a criminal offense.

14

B. State of Mind

The second essential element of a crime is the state of mind or *mens rea*. *Mens rea* encompasses notions of a guilty mind, a wrongful purpose, and criminal intent. The extent to which a person may be held criminally responsible for his or her actions generally depends upon the nature of the mental state under which the person was laboring at the time of the act in question.

Understand the various states of mind. The Texas statute provides a good example with the four levels: purposeful, knowing, reckless, and negligent. Define each level. Distinguish between general intent and specific intent. Specific intent crimes usually involve a secondary purpose; that is, the perpetrator commits one crime with the intent to commit another. The term "scienter" is used to signify a defendant's knowledge or "guilty knowledge."

The special category of strict liability crimes require no culpable mental state and presents a significant exception to the principle that all crimes require a conjunction of action and state of mind. Routine traffic offenses are generally considered as strict liability offenses.

C. Concurrence

Concurrence requires that the act and the mental state occur together in order for a crime to take place. If one precedes the other and does not exist at any time with the other, no criminal act has occurred.

Capstone Cases: Learning Issues

United States v. *Hanousek*

1. Hanousek assigned as error the failure of the trial court to instruct the jury that the government had to prove "criminal negligence" as opposed to "ordinary negligence." What is the difference between the two types of negligence?

2. Where did the Court first look in determining the meaning of the statute involved in the case?

3. How did the Court ascertain the intent of Congress in passing the statute?

4. May a public welfare statute subject a person to criminal liability for his or her ordinary negligence? If so, why?

5. What was the Court's conclusion regarding the trial court's instructions to the jury?

People v. *Jensen*

1. Why did the Supreme Court return the case to the appellate court for reconsideration?

2. What specific acts of the defendant were alleged to have constituted the crime?

3. Is the crime involved a mala in se or mala prohibita crime? Explain.

4. Why did the defendant contend that the statute in question was unconstitutional?

5. How did the Court determine the intent of the legislature in passing the statute?

Cheek v. *United States*

1. Upon what grounds did the defendant base his contentions that he was not required to pay federal income tax?

2. If the defendant "honestly and reasonably believed" that he was not required to pay the tax, would this be a defense to the prosecution? Explain your answer.

3. Why is "ignorance of the law" generally not a defense in a criminal case?

4. How did the Court define "willfulness" in this case?

5. Why did Justices Blackmun and Marshall disagree with the other justices?

People v. *Ryan*

1. What was the key issue in the Ryan case?

2. How did the Appellate Division define the term "knowingly?"

3. Why did the Supreme Court reversed the Appellate Division?

4. Explain the Supreme Court's holding regarding the statutory construction of the crime that would have made the crime a "strict liability" crime.

PRACTICE TEST QUESTIONS

MULTIPLE CHOICE

___ 2.1.   In a criminal case, the prosecution has the burden of proving the defendant guilty by
a. clear and convincing evidence.
b. a preponderance of evidence.
c. proof beyond a reasonable doubt.
d. proof beyond a substantial doubt.

___ 2.2.   A ____ can mean a probability of just over 50 percent that the defendant did what is claimed.
a. preponderance of the evidence
b. clear and convincing evidence
c. proof beyond a substantial doubt
d. certainty of the evidence

___ 2.3.   The essence of crime consists of three conjoined and essential elements: the criminal act, a culpable mental state, and
a. sufficient evidence.
b. proof beyond a reasonable doubt.
c. *means rea.*
d. a concurrence of the two.

___ 2.4.   The culpable mental state of a crime is termed the
a. *actus reus.*
b. *mens rea.*
c. *corpus dilecti.*
d. *motive.*

___ 2.5.   The ____ means in Latin a "guilty act."
a. *actus reus*
b. *mens rea*
c. *corpus dilecti*
d. *motive*

___ 2.6.   An individual who does not have actual custody of an item but has control or influence over it is said to exercise ____ possession over the item.
a. constructive
b. mere
c. actual
d. knowing

___ 2.7.   The term _____ literally means "guilty mind."
        a. *actus reus*
        b. *mens rea*
        c. *corpus dilecti*
        d. *motive*

___ 2.8.   Which of the mental states below cannot serve as the basis for criminal liability?
        a. knowing
        b. reckless
        c. pure accident
        d. negligent

___ 2.9.   Risk of such nature and degree that the failure to perceive it constitutes a gross deviation from the standard of conduct constitutes
        a. purposeful action.
        b. mere negligence.
        c. criminal negligence.
        d. simple negligence.

___ 2.10.   Intent that refers to an actor's physical conduct and is that form of intent that can be assumed from the defendant's behavior constitutes
        a. specific intent.
        b. general intent.
        c. transferred intent.
        d. purposeful intent.

___ 2.11.   The thoughtful conscious intention to perform an act constitutes
        a. specific intent.
        b. general intent.
        c. transferred intent.
        d. purposeful intent.

___ 2.12.   The term _____ is sometimes used to signify a defendant's guilty knowledge.
        a. scienter
        b. general intent
        c. specific intent
        d. *mens rea*

___ 2.13.   The _____ is a person's reason for committing a crime.
        a. intent
        b. *mens rea*
        c. purpose
        d. motive

___ 2.14.   Statutory rape is generally considered as a(n) _____ offense.
a. general intent
b. strict liability
c. specific intent
d. purposeful intent

___ 2.15.   The adversarial system has its origins in the ancient practice of trial by
a. fire.
b. the church.
c. combat.
d. by ordeal.

___ 2.16.   The Model Code of Professional Responsibility was created by the
a. federal government.
b. state bar associations.
c. American Bar Association.
d. Trial Lawyers Association.

___ 2.17.   The U.S. Supreme Court in the _____ case held that the reasonable doubt standard plays a vital role in the American scheme of criminal procedure.
a. *Morissette* v. *United States*
b. *United States* v. *Behrman*
c. *People* v. *Reisman*
d. *In re Winship*

___ 2.18.   The term _____ may be used to describe the degree of blameworthiness assigned to the defendant after processing by a court.
a. purposeful intent
b. criminal liability
c. knowing behavior
d. willful behavior

___ 2.19.   Action undertaken with an awareness is considered as
a. purposeful intent.
b. criminal liability.
c. knowing behavior.
d. willful behavior.

___ 2.20.   A person engages in conduct _____ if he engages in the conduct in plain, conscious, and unjustifiable disregard of the harm that might result.
a. knowingly
b. recklessly
c. intentionally
d. purposefully

___ 2.21. The prosecution has the burden of proving by clear and convincing evidence each element of an offense before the defendant may be convicted of that offense.

___ 2.22. The adversarial system requires that advocates for both sides do their utmost, within the boundaries set by law and professional ethics, to protect and advance the interests of their clients.

___ 2.23. The U.S. Supreme Court in the *In re Winship* case clearly defined the "proof beyond a reasonable doubt" standard.

___ 2.24. Central to the adversarial system is the advocacy model.

___ 2.25. The American Bar Association may discipline attorneys who violate their codes of professional conduct.

___ 2.26. For conduct to be criminal, there must be a concurrence between the criminal act and the culpable mental state.

___ 2.27. In criminal law, the term "conduct" encompasses both behavior and one's mental state that was present at the time of the behavior.

___ 2.28. All statutes defining criminal activity also specify the required *mens rea*.

___ 2.29. A person's state of mind is usually inferred from a person's actions and from all the surrounding circumstances.

___ 2.30. Most strict liability offenses are violations of regulatory statutes.

KEY CONCEPTS

Identify the below key concepts from Chapter 2 of the text:

_____ 2.1. The simultaneous coexistence of an act in violation of the law and a culpable mental state.

_____ 2.2. A person's reason for committing a crime.

_____ 2.3. Liability without fault or intention.

_____ 2.4. Directions given by a judge to the jury concerning the law of the case.

_____ 2.5. In-court arrangement that pit the prosecution against the defense in the belief that truth can best be realized through effective debate over the merits of the opposing sides.

_____ 2.6. The degree of blameworthiness assigned to a defendant by a criminal court and the concomitant extent to which the defendant is subject to penalties prescribed by the criminal law.

_____ 2.7. The basic components of crime; in a specific crime, the essential features of that crime as specified by law or statute.

_____ 2.8. A guilty act.

_____ 2.9. Possession of a substance in which one may or may not be aware of what he or she possesses.

_____ 2.10. An intentional or unintentional failure to act, which may impose criminal liability if a duty to act under the circumstances is specified by law.

_____ 2.11. Possession of a substance in which one has direct physical control over the substance.

_____ 2.12. The specific mental state operative in the defendant at the time of a crime; a guilty mind.

_____ 2.13. Those particular forms of voluntary behavior that are prohibited by law.

_____ 2.14. A thoughtful, conscious intention to perform a specific act in order to achieve a particular result.

_____ 2.15. That form of intent that can be assumed from the defendant's behavior.

_____ 2.16. Knowledge; guilty knowledge.

_____ 2.17. Action undertaken with awareness.

_____ 2.18. That which is undertaken volitionally to achieve some goal.

_____ 2.19. The flagrant and reckless disregard for the safety of others.

_____ 2.20. The ability to exercise control over property and objects, even though they are not in one's physical custody.

FACTUAL SCENARIOS

1. Jerry is the owner of a large company. For some reason, the company trucks are not properly registered with the state. Jerry does not take an active part in the management of the company. Jerry is issued a citation for the failure to register the company vehicles, an infraction. Should he be held accountable for the failure of his company to register the vehicles? Would your answer be any different if the county proceeded against him in a civil rather than a criminal court? Explain your answers.

2. Harvey farms a large farm in California. His fields have recently been planted with seed grain. Birds are flocking to the fields and eating the seeds. Having watched the movie "Steel Magnolias," he decides to scare the birds off by shooting at them. Harvey orders four of his employees to take their guns and go out to the fields and shoot the birds. He instructs the employees to make a lot of noise. Jorge, one of the employees, takes a couple of shots with a shotgun at the birds. He kills three of the birds. A game warden arrives on the scene and cites Jorge for hunting without a license, a misdemeanor. Should Jorge be convicted of hunting without a license? Explain your answer.

CROSSWORD 2

Across

5. Guilty knowledge

8. That which is used to prove facts

10. Held responsible

12. The criminal act

14. Generally a person must commit some ___ before he or she is subject to criminal liability.

15. Behavior which increases the risk of harm

16. Liability without fault

17. That form of intent that can be assumed from the defendant's voluntary conduct

19. Our system of prosecution

20. Action which is undertaken volitionally to achieve some goal

Down

1. The party with the duty of proving a fact has the ___ of proof.

2. Crimes require both an act and a particular state of ___.

3. A thoughtful, conscious intention to perform a specific act in order to achieve a particular result

4. The ___ of the defendant is determined by the jury in a jury trial.

6. Behavior

7. The reason for committing a crime

9. The basic components of a crime

11. Possession with an awareness of what the item is that is possessed

13. There must be a ___ of the act and the state of mind.

14. That type of possession in which one has direct physical control over the object

18. Possession with or without an awareness of the nature of the item

Chapter 3

Expanding the Concept of Crime

CHAPTER SUMMARY

I. Introduction

Study the text regarding the court case involving David Smith and the trial court's holding that in order for the State to establish *corpus delicti* it must provide evidence that the burning was a willful act and not a result of natural or accidental causes.

II. *Corpus Delicti*

Corpus delicti means "body of crime." To establish it, the prosecution must establish that a criminal law has been violated, and that someone violated it. It has two components that a certain result has been produced and that a person is criminally responsible. Understand the concept that a criminal conviction cannot be based solely on the uncorroborated confession or admission of the accused. The *corpus delicti* is also important because it is necessary to establish where a crime is committed because of the requirement for the crime to be prosecuted in the judicial district where the crime was committed. Federal courts and a few states have abandoned the requirement of establishing the *corpus delicti* because doing so is not always possible.

III. Additional Elements of Crime

The traditional view is that the three features of crime discussed in the last chapter are sufficient to describe the essence of the legal concept of crime. Other scholars argue for four additional principles. Those principles are causation, a resulting harm, the principle of legality, and necessary attendant circumstances.

A. Causation

Causation refers to the fact that the concurrence of a guilty mind and a criminal act must produce or cause harm. The word "causes" is open to a number of interpretations. It is necessary to understand the difference between causation in fact and proximate cause. If there is a factual link between the actor's conduct and the resulting harm, causation in fact exists. A cause in fact may not be the sole or even the primary cause.

The idea of proximate cause is more useful in criminal law than factual cause. Proximate cause holds individuals criminally liable for causing harm when it can logically be shown that the harm caused was reasonably foreseeable from their conduct. Proximate cause is also the primary cause. Proximate cause requires some direct relation between the injury asserted and the injurious conduct alleged. The ALI suggests the use of the term legal cause rather than proximate cause. Legal causes can be distinguished from those causes which may have produced the result in question, but which may not provide the basis for a criminal prosecution because they are too complex, too indistinguishable from other causes, not knowable, or not provable in a court of law.

B. Resulting Harm

Understand the need for identifiable harm as a general feature of crime. Also discuss victimless crimes or social order offenses and the element of harm. The question is whether the defendant's conduct caused the harm which the law in question sought to prevent. The need of an identifiable harm is sometimes specified by law as an element of an offense. Other times, degree of harm increases the seriousness of an offense. When a particular result is specified as a necessary element of a crime, successful prosecution requires both a concurrence of *mens rea* and the act, as well as of *mens rea* and the resulting harm.

The felony murder rule is an exception to the general notion that criminal liability does not accrue when the harm that results is different in kind from the harm intended. Harm means loss, disadvantage, or injury or anything so regarded by the person affected, including loss, disadvantage, or injury to any person in whose welfare he or she is interested.

C. The Principle of Legality

The principle of legality reflects the fact that behavior cannot be criminal if no law exists which both defines it as illegal and prescribes a punishment for it. There is no crime and, thus, no punishment without a law. The principle also includes the notion that a law cannot be created tomorrow which will hold a person legally responsible for something he or she does today. Another aspect of the principle is the constitutional void-for-vagueness principle, i.e., a statue which either forbids or requires the doing of an act in terms so vague that men of common intelligence must necessarily guess at its meaning and differ as to its application. Statutes are void when vague because their enforcement would require interpretations of which fact situations the law applies.

D. Necessary Attendant Circumstances

Attendant circumstances specified by law as necessary elements of an offense are referred to as necessary attendant circumstances. Attendant circumstances refer to the facts surrounding the event. Often the attendant circumstances increase the degree or level of seriousness of an offense. They can also be classified as aggravating or mitigating, and may, by law, be used to lessen or increase the penalty that can be imposed upon a convicted offender.

CAPSTONE CASES: LEARNING ISSUES

Johnson v. *State*

    1.   What is meant by the term "the *corpus deliciti* of a crime?"

    2.   Why is the prosecution required to establish the *corpus deliciti* of a crime?

    3.   What is the statutory definition of robbery in Indiana as set forth in a footnote to the decision?

Chicago v. *Morales*

    1.   Define "loitering."

    2.   What are the reasons that "vagueness" may invalidate a criminal law?

    3.   What was the city's response to the concern about "adequate notice" issue?

    4.   What's wrong with an ordinance that gives discretion to the police?

PRACTICE TEST QUESTIONS

MULTIPLE CHOICE

____ 3.1.   The term *corpus delicti* literally means
        a. elements of the crime.
        b. dead body.
        c. body of crime.
        d. judicial death.

____ 3.2.   There are only ____ components of the *corpus delicti* of a crime.
        a. two
        b. three
        c. four
        d. five

____ 3.3.   It is a principle of law in most jurisdictions that a mere extrajudicial confession, uncorroborated by other facts, is insufficient to establish the ____, and cannot support a conviction.
        a. *mens rea*
        b. *corpus juris*
        c. *corpus delicti*
        d. *actus rea*

___ 3.4.   Causation refers to the fact that the concurrence of a guilty mind and a criminal act must
a. cause harm.
b. jointly exist.
c. exist separately.
d. cause concern.

___ 3.5.   The first cause in a string of events that ultimately produced the harm in question is the
a. proximate cause.
b. causation in fact.
c. proximate results.
d. causation in law.

___ 3.6.   The U.S. Supreme Court has observed that ____ requires some direct relation between the injury asserted and the injurious conduct alleged.
a. proximate cause
b. causation in fact
c. proximate results
d. causation in law

___ 3.7.   The phrase *nullen crimen, nulla poena, sine lege* means:
a. no crime without punishment.
b. there is no crime, there is no punishment, without law.
c. sanctions may lawfully be imposed.
d. sanctions may not be lawfully imposed.

___ 3.8.   It is permissible to drink beer, if you are of the "drinking age," because there is no statute prohibiting it; this illustrates the principle of
a. causation.
b. harm.
c. legality.
d. retrospective.

___ 3.9.   Statutes in defining crimes may specify that additional elements or ____ be present in order for a conviction to be obtained.
a. attendant circumstances
b. necessary restrictions
c. causation in fact
d. additional intent

___ 3.10.   Aggravating and ____ circumstances are not elements of an offense, since they are primarily relevant at the sentencing stage of a criminal trial.
a. motivation

b. mitigating

c. additional

d. necessary

TRUE/FALSE

____ 3.11. The term *corpus delicti* literally means the "location of the body."

____ 3.12. In most jurisdictions, an extrajudicial confession, uncorroborated by other facts, is insufficient to support a conviction.

____ 3.13. Causation does not require that the concurrence of a guilty mind and a criminal act produce or cause harm.

____ 3.14. The terms "causation in fact" and "proximate cause" are similar in concept and may be used interchangeably.

____ 3.15. Factual causation may be determined through the *sine qua non* test.

____ 3.16. Proof of factual cause is necessary for a conviction.

____ 3.17. Proof of factual cause is sufficient for a conviction to result.

____ 3.18. Proximate cause is also a primary cause.

____ 3.19. The concept of "legal cause" is used to indicate that a cause must be close in time and space to the result it produces.

____ 3.20. The need for some identifiable harm is often cited as a general feature of crime.

KEY CONCEPTS

Identify the below key concepts from Chapter 3 of the text:

_____ 3.1. The body of the crime.

_____ 3.2. A principle of law that says that an out-of-court confession, unsupported by other facts, is insufficient to support a criminal conviction.

_____ 3.3. An actual link between an actor's conduct and a result.

_____ 3.4. The type of cause that is required to be demonstrated in court in order to hold an individual criminally liable for causing harm.

_____ 3.5. The primary or moving cause that plays a substantial part in bringing about injury or damage.

_____ 3.6. An axiom that holds that behavior cannot be criminal if no law exists that defines it as such.

_____ 3.7 A method for determining causality which holds that "without this, that would not be."

_____ 3.8. The facts surrounding an event.

_____ 3.9. A constitutional principle that refers to a statute defining a crime that is so unclear that a reasonable person of at least average intelligence could not determine what the law purports to command or prohibit.

_____ 3.10. Formulated, enacted, or operating retrospectively.

FACTUAL SCENARIOS

1. Joe, intending to kill his wife Joan, purchased a hunting knife. He also takes out a large life insurance policy on her with himself as the beneficiary. Later, he feels ashamed of his actions and hides the knife on a top shelf in the bedroom closet. Joan, while hunting for a missing shoe, reaches over her head to the top shelf and causes the knife to fall. The knife strikes her in the head. Seriously hurt, she calls the police. The police attempt to transport her to the hospital. On the way to the hospital, the ambulance is hit by a drunk driver and she is killed. When Joe hears that his wife has been killed, he goes to the local bar and celebrates. Should Joe be held accountable for his wife's death?

2. A state defines one type of "indecent exposure" as exposing one's genitals in public. There is no mention of any required mental state. What are the elements of this offense? Paul is walking down the street. His trousers are unzipped. Part of his genitals are exposed. Paul admits that when stopped by the police, his trousers were unzipped and part of his genitals were exposed. He testified, however, that he did not know that the trousers were unzipped. The judge believes his testimony. Is he guilty of indecent exposure? Apply the facts to the crime. Discuss your conclusions.

3. Defendant Banks was charged with violating the State's "Peeping Tom" statute, which made punishable "any person who shall peep secretly into any room occupied by a female." Banks contended that the statute was unconstitutionally vague because men or common intelligence must necessarily guess at its meaning and differ as to its application. He also contended that the statute prohibited innocent conduct. Was the statute unconstitutionally vague? [See: _In Re Banks_, 244 S.E. 2nd 386 (1978).]

CROSSWORD 3

Across

3. The level of seriousness of an offense

6. ___ law specifies a number of degrees of sexual battery.

9. The U.S. ___

10. Ex post ___

11. Consumption by minors is illegal.

12. The state whose statutes classify burglary in two degrees

14. ___ Marie Reynolds

15. Sexual ____

18. The __ for rule

19. ___ delicti

20. ___ crimen sine poena

21. The degree of ___ is higher if the building is inhabited.

Down

1. The corpus ___ of the crime

2. The causation in ___ refers to an actual link between an actor's conduct and a result.

4. The ___ harm

5. The primary cause

7. The principle of ____

8. ___ circumstances refer to the facts surrounding an event.

9. The fact that the concurrence of a guilty mind and a criminal act may produce harm

13. ___ battery

16. Illegal

17. The type of cause that is required to be demonstrated in court in order to hold an individual criminally liable for causing harm

Chapter 4

Extending Criminal Liability:
Inchoate Offenses and Parties to Crime

CHAPTER SUMMARY

I. Introduction

Inchoate offenses are incipient crimes that generally lead to other crimes. They are also referred to as anticipatory offenses. Traditionally they include attempts, solicitation, and conspiracies. Understand the conceptual difficulty with inchoate crimes in that the earlier the police intervene, the greater the possibility that the person will be arrested for innocent conduct. Some inchoate crimes are often thought of as complete crimes. They are inchoate crimes in disguise. Such crimes include burglary and the possession of burglary tools.

II. Criminal Attempt

Understand the six stages necessary for a person to intentionally commit an offense and how attempt is not completed until the middle stages. Statutory definitions of attempt are generally brief and fail to provide a complete understanding as to what constitutes an attempt. Generally to go from mere preparation to an attempt there must be an act that constitutes a substantial step toward the commission of the intended offense. Attempt is a specific intent crime. The elements of the crime of attempt are (1) a specific intent to commit a criminal offense and (2) a substantial step undertaken toward the commission of the intended offense.

A. The Act Requirement

To constitute an attempt, an act of some sort is necessary. Mere preparation to commit an offense is not sufficient to support a charge of attempt. Some specific action must be taken toward the actual completion of the intended offense.

B. Preparation

The Model Penal Code provides that conduct is not an attempt unless it involves a substantial step toward the commission of the intended offense and is strongly corroborative of the actor's criminal purpose. The tests that the courts have used include the last act test, physical proximity test, and the dangerous proximity test.

The proximity approach was the traditional test used at common law. Under this test any acts remotely leading toward the commission of the offense are not considered as attempts to commit the crime, but acts immediately connected with it are. This approach is based on the last-act test which originated in England. The last-act test requires that the accused has taken the last step or act and has performed all that he intended to do and was able to do in an attempt to commit the crime. The test was abandoned because of the claim that it made it virtually impossible for law enforcement personnel to prevent the commission of a substantive crime.

The physical proximity test was an effort to reduce the strict provisions of the last act test. Under the physical proximity test, the substantial step need not be the last act, but it must approach sufficiently near to it in order to stand as a substantial step in the direct movement toward the commission of the intended offense.

Justice Oliver Wendell Holmes developed the dangerous proximity test. This test incorporates the physical proximity standard but is more flexible. Thus, a person is guilty of an attempt under the test when his or her conduct is in dangerous proximity to success.

Alternatives to the proximity approach include the indispensable element test, the unequivocally test, and the probable desistance test. Under the indispensable element test, the accused is not guilty of an attempt if he or she has yet to obtain control of an indispensable feature of the crime. Under the unequivocally test, an act does not become an attempt until it ceases to be equivocal. Under the probable desistance approach, the defendant's conduct constitutes an attempt if it has gone beyond the point where the defendant is likely to voluntarily stop short of completing the offense.

The Model Penal Code approach uses the substantial step test. This approach is used in most states and the federal courts. It incorporates aspects of the proximity test and the unequivocally test. Any conduct that meets any of the variations of either test is sufficient to constitute an attempt.

C. Defenses

Anyone charged with an attempt may generally raise two defenses: abandonment and impossibility. The defense of abandonment claims that the defendant voluntarily decided to renounce continued attempts to commit the crime. Abandonment is an affirmative defense. Postponement of the crime because of police intervention, weather, a debilitating accident, or some other inability to continue is not a bar to prosecution.

The defense of impossibility may be either factual or legal variety. Factual impossibility claims that the defendant could not have committed the envisioned offense even if he or she had been able to carry through the attempt to do so. In most situations factual impossibility is not a valid defense. Legal impossibility generally precludes prosecution in most jurisdictions. The legal impossibility claims that the attempted offense is really no offense at all.

D. Completed Offense

An attempt is generally a lessor included offense of the intended offense. If the crime is completed, however, then the attempt is merged into the completed offense and the defendant is guilty of the substantive offense, and not both the offense and the attempt. Generally, however, the fact that the substantive offense was completed is not a defense to an indictment or complaint alleging only an attempt.

E. Punishment

At common law, attempts were punished as misdemeanors. Generally, attempts are punished less severely than completed crimes. The punishment schemes relating to attempts are usually related to the grading system established for the intended offense.

III. Criminal Conspiracy

A criminal conspiracy is an agreement between two or more persons to commit or to effect the commission of an unlawful act, or to use unlawful means to accomplish an act that is not unlawful. Conspiracy was first formulated by the English Star Chamber in 1611. There appears to be an enormous growth in the number of conspiracy cases prosecuted in the last two decades. In addition, there is an increase in the complexity of the cases.

A. Doctrine of Complicity

Conspiracy is a complex and controversial crime. It gives prosecutors a broad authority to charge individuals for what often appear to be rather nebulous offenses. Some contend that there is a greater risk that persons will be punished for what they think rather than what they do.

B. Elements of the Crime

The elements of criminal conspiracy are as follows:
   I.   An agreement between two or more persons.
   II. To carry out an act which is unlawful or which is lawful, but to be accomplished by unlawful means.
   III. A culpable intent on the part of the defendants.

C. Plurality Requirement

The essence of the crime of conspiracy is an agreement for the joint purpose of unlawful ends. It necessarily involves two or more persons. The required agreement does not need to be a meeting of the minds as is required for an enforceable contract. All that is needed is for the parties to communicate to each other in some way their intentions to pursue a joint and criminal objective, or to pursue a joint objective in a criminal manner. An implied agreement is sufficient.

Wharton's Rule provides that where the targeted crime by its very nature takes more than one person to commit, then there can be no conspiracy when no more than the number of persons required to commit the offense participate in it. Wharton's Rule has not been incorporated into the Model Penal Code.

D. Required Intent

To constitute conspiracy, there must be some intent on the part of the conspirators to reach an agreement, and there must be an intent to achieve the objective. Some states require a corrupt motive. Most states do not require that the conspirators act with an evil purpose.

E. Parties to a Conspiracy

There is no requirement that each party form an agreement with all of the other parties involved in the conspiracy. The parties may not know one another and may not even be aware of the involvement of all of the other parties. Two common elaborate type conspiracies are the wheel and chain conspiracies.

F. Duration of Conspiracy

Generally, a conspiracy continues until the crime it anticipates is either completed or is abandoned by all of the parties involved. It is often important to establish when an individual conspirator withdrew for a variety of purposes. To effectively constitute a withdrawal, the individual generally must give notice of having withdrawn to other conspirators or to law enforcement officials. The defendant must show that the withdrawal was voluntary for it to be a defense.

IV. Criminal Solicitation

Criminal solicitation occurs when one person requests or encourages another person to perform a criminal act. All states have codified the crime of criminal solicitation. It requires no overt act. It does require a mental state such that the defendant must have intended to induce another person to commit a crime. There is no requirement that the solicited crime be committed or even that the other party agrees to commit the crime.

V. Parties to Crime

Common law had a complex scheme of labeling persons involved in a felony according to their relationship to the criminal act. The principal in the first degree was the individual who personally performed the act; the principal in the second degree was the person who as present at crime scene and aided or abetted the commission of the offenses; an accessory before the fact was a person who was not present at the crime scene but who aided or abetted the crime; an accessory after the fact was a person who furnished post-crime assistance to the accused.

A. Relationship of Complicity

Modern law does not distinguish between the principal in the second degree and an accessory before the fact. Presently, the degree of criminal liability is rarely dependent upon one's presence or absence at the crime scene. One who assists in the commission of a crime, but does not commit the act is considered as an accomplice or an accessory. The individual who actually commits the criminal act is considered as the principal. The principal and accomplices are said to have a relationship of complicity.

B. Accomplice Liability

Accomplice liability is based on the concept that any person who aids, abets, encourages, or assists another person to commit a crime should share in the criminal liability which accrues under law. Words alone may be sufficient. Mere presence at the crime scene is not, by itself, sufficient to render one an accomplice.

C. Accessory

An accessory is an individual who gives assistance to a person who has committed a felony for the purposes of helping that individual avoid apprehension or detection. Guilt requires a showing that a felony has been completed, that the defendant knew that it was committed by the individual who was being assisted, and assistance must have been given personally to the felon. It is not necessary for the accessory to be aware of the precise details of the crime. At common law, the crime of misprison of a felony was the failure to report a known felony. In most cases, mere failure to inform authorities of an offender's presence or failure to come forward is not sufficient to make a person an accessory after the fact.

D. The Criminal Liability of Corporations

The modern trend is to hold corporations criminally liable for illegal acts performed by agents acting on behalf of the corporations. This is especially true for strict liability crimes and minor offenses. Understand the situations wherein the Model Penal Code would hold a corporation criminally liable.

E. Vicarious Liability

Vicarious liability is related to strict liability. It imposes criminal liability on one party for the criminal acts of another party. It is generally associated only with regulatory crimes, and the most common form of vicarious liability is that of an employer who is held liable for the criminal acts of employees.

CAPSTONE CASES: LEARNING ISSUES

Tennessee v. *Reeves*

     1.   What is the specific issue before the court?

     2.   Explain the "overt act" requirement of an attempt.

     3.   What constitutes a "substantial step" under the Tennessee statute on attempts?

     4.   Does the jury or the judge make the determination as to whether the defendant's conduct constitutes a "substantial step" under the statute?

     5.   Why did the court abandon the "Dupuy rule?"

New Hampshire v. *Allcock*

     1.   What conduct of the defendant's constituted a "substantial step" towards commission of the crime?

     2.   What did the defendant need in order to prevail on her claim that there was insufficient evidence to convict?

     3.   Why did the court consider that the proper focus of the inquiry was to determine whether defendant's conduct "strongly corroborated a clear criminal intent?

State v. *Kobe*:

     1.   What is required under Missouri law to convict another of being an accomplice?

     2.   Why wasn't the defendant's presence at the crime sufficient to convict him?

     3.   What were the facts that convinced the court of the defendant's guilt?

People v. *Eubanks*

     1.   Why did the defendant contend that the evidence did not establish his guilt beyond reasonable doubt of aggravated battery with a firearm and armed robbery?

2. Why did the defendant maintain that he could not be held accountable for the armed robbery?

3. What did the court mean by the statement that a "rational trier of fact could have concluded that defendant was accountable for the shooting of Macon?"

Commonwealth v. *McIlwain School Bus Lines*

1. What was the principle issue in the case?

2. What was meant by the statement "from an order quashing an information?"

3. What is the general rule today regarding holding a corporation liable for crimes?

4. How did the court determine that a corporation was a "person" within the meaning of the code?

PRACTICE TEST QUESTIONS

MULTIPLE CHOICE

___ 4.1. Incipient crimes which generally lead to other crimes are called ____ offenses.
a. conceptual
b. premature
c. predatory
d. inchoate

___ 4.2. Which of the below listed crimes is not considered an inchoate offense?
a. burglary
b. possession of burglary tools
c. stalking
d. criminal homicide

___ 4.3. The federal courts use the ___ test to determine if the conduct in question constitutes an attempt.
a. substantial step
b. last step
c. close proximity
d. nearest

___ 4.4. Generally speaking, courts have held that ___ to commit an offense is not sufficient to support a charge of attempted criminal activity.
a. mere preparation
b. substantial steps

c. substantial conduct

d. substantial preparation

___ 4.5.   When considering criminal attempts, the proximity test is based on the ___ test.

a. substantial step

b. last act

c. dangerous proximity

d. physical proximity

___ 4.6.   In an effort to reduce the strict provisions of the last act test for criminal attempts, the ____ test was developed.

a. substantial step

b. last act

c. dangerous proximity

d. physical proximity

___ 4.7.   The ____ test incorporates the physical proximity standard but is more flexible.

a. substantial step

b. last act

c. dangerous proximity

d. last physical proximity

___ 4.8.   Under the ____ test for criminal attempts, an act does not become an attempt until it ceases to be equivocal.

a. dangerous proximity

b. indispensable element

c. last step

d. unequivocal

___ 4.9.   In regard to criminal attempts, the Model Penal Code uses the ___ test.

a. substantial step

b. last act

c. dangerous proximity

d. last physical proximity

___ 4.10.   The defense of ___ claims that the defendant voluntarily decided to renounce continued attempts to commit the crime.

a. impossibility

b. renunciation

c. abandonment

d. Answers b. and c. are both correct.

___ 4.11.   Trying to kill someone who is already dead is considered as a ___ impossibility.

a. factual

b. legal

c. moral

d. legal and factual

____ 4.12.   In a ___ conspiracy, the conspirators deal only with a ring leader and not each other.

a. wheel

b. chain

c. hub

d. wagon

____ 4.13.   In the ___ type of conspiracy, the conspiracy involves a sequence of individuals.

a. wheel

b. chain

c. hub

d. wagon

____ 4.14.   Generally speaking, a conspiracy continues until the crime is

a. completed.

b. abandoned by all of the parties involved.

c. attempted.

d. Both a. and b. above are correct.

____ 4.15.   For a defense of withdrawal to conspiracy to be successful, the defendant must establish that the withdrawal was voluntary and that the

a. success of the conspiracy was thwarted.

b. other defendants confessed.

c. other defendants were the leaders of the conspiracy.

d. other defendants were caught.

____ 4.16.   The common law crime of ____ occurs when one person requests or encourages another to perform a criminal act.

a. criminal conspiracy

b. criminal solicitation

c. attempt

d. bribery

____ 4.17.   One major difference between conspiracy and criminal solicitation is that

a. conspiracy requires no special mental state.

b. criminal solicitation requires no special mental state.

c. conspiracy requires no overt act.

d. criminal solicitation requires no overt act.

____ 4.18.   At common law, the individual who personally performed the criminal act was considered the

a. principal in the first degree.

b. principal in the second degree.

c. accessory before the fact.

d. accessory after the fact.

___ 4.19. Any person who aids, abets, encourages, or assists another person to commit a crime is a(n)

a. principal.

b. accomplice.

c. accessory after the fact.

d. None of the above choices are correct.

___ 4.20. Vicarious liability is a concept that is generally associated only with ___ crimes.

a. personal

b. regulatory

c. property

d. victimless

TRUE/FALSE

___ 4.21. Burglary is an inchoate crime.

___ 4.22. The defense of abandonment is an affirmative defense and most jurisdictions do not require that the abandonment be voluntary.

___ 4.23. The defense of impossibility may be either factual or legal impossibility.

___ 4.24. Factual impossibility is rarely a successful defense.

___ 4.25. The defense of legal impossibility claims that the attempted offense is really no offense at all.

___ 4.26. If the defendant is charged with an attempt, he or she cannot be convicted on evidence that the offense was actually committed.

___ 4.27. At common law, all attempts were punished as felonies.

___ 4.28. A criminal conspiracy is an agreement between two or more persons to commit or to effect the commission of an unlawful act, or to use unlawful means to accomplish an act that is not unlawful.

___ 4.29. Conspiracy is a complex, but non-controversial, crime.

___ 4.30 In a conspiracy, the law does not require that each party form an agreement with all the parties involved.

KEY CONCEPTS

Identify the below key concepts from Chapter 4 of the text:

_____ 4.1. An unfinished crime that generally leads to another crime.

_____ 4.2. Significant activity undertaken in furtherance of some goal.

_____ 4.3. Preparatory actions taken toward a crime that are remote from the actual commission of the crime.

_____ 4.4. A test for assessing attempts, under which a person is guilty of an attempt when his or her conduct comes dangerously close to success.

_____ 4.5. A test traditionally used under common law to determine whether a person was guilty of attempted criminal activity.

_____ 4.6. A defense to a charge of attempted criminal activity.

_____ 4.7. A defense to a charge of attempted criminal activity that claims that defendant could not have factually or legally committed the envisioned offense even if he or she had been able to carry through the attempt to do so.

_____ 4.8. A rule applicable to conspiracy cases that holds that, when the targeted crime by its very nature takes more than one person to commit, then there can be no conspiracy when no more than the number of persons required to commit the offense participate in it.

_____ 4.9. The voluntary and complete abandonment of the intent and purpose to commit a criminal offense.

_____ 4.10. All parties who take part in the commission of a crime.

_____ 4.11. An agreement between two or more persons to effect the commission of an unlawful act.

_____ 4.12. Any one who aid and abets in the commission of a crime, but who was not present at the crime scene.

_____ 4.13. The logical and legal requirement that a conspiracy involve two or more parties.

_____ 4.14. The encouraging, requesting, or commanding of another person to commit a crime.

_____ 4.15. A person who furnishes post-crime assistance to keep the offender from being detected or from being arrested.

_____ 4.16. The failure to report a known crime.

_____ 4.17. The criminal liability of one party for the criminal acts or another party.

_____ 4.18. An anticipatory crime.

FACTUAL SCENARIOS

1. Jerry needed money to pay his medical school tuition. He decided to rob the First National Bank of New York. He asked his classmate Kenn to help him. They agreed to split the take: 40 percent for Kenn and 60 percent for Jerry. This arrangement was based on the fact that Kenn was only going to purchase the gun and a ski mask for Jerry and was going to be a lookout at the bank. Kenn purchased a .38 revolver and a ski mask. After purchasing the items on Wednesday, Kenn stopped in the local bar for a couple of drinks. There he bragged to Paul about the planned crime and asked Paul if he would join in the planned robbery. Paul, an undercover police officer, agreed to take part in the robbery. The robbery was planned for Thursday evening. Later Wednesday evening, Kenn and Jerry met for dinner. During dinner, they were arrested. As the newly elected district attorney, what crimes can you charge Jerry and Kenn with? Does their action constitute the crime of attempt? Explain your answers.

2. Paul and his wife Susan were getting a divorce. Paul was unhappy that Susan would be getting a substantial portion of the family property. He resolved to kill her by poisoning her. He went to the drug store complaining of insomnia. The druggist gave him a bottle of non-prescription sleeping pills. Paul, mistakenly believing these pills to be lethal in quantity, placed 30 tablets into his wife's coffee. She drank the coffee, but suffered no ill effects except mild drowsiness. Paul is charged with attempted murder. Evidence indicated that even ingesting 100 pills simultaneously would not have killed a person. Paul is charged with attempted murder. May he be convicted of that crime? Explain your answer.

CROSSWORD 4

Across

2. An agreement to commit an offense

4. The relationship of ____

5. __ preparation insufficient to constitute an attempt

9. This defense claims that the defendant voluntarily decided to renounce continued attempts to commit the crime.

10. Wharton's ___

11. ___ after the fact

12. Encouraging another person to commit a crime

14. The defense of abandonment

15. A person who aids, promotes, or contributes to the completion of the crime

17. ___ proximity test

18. To constitute an attempt, the actor must take a ___ step toward the commission of the intended offense.

Down

1. Criminal liability of one party for the acts of another party

3. ____ of a felony

6. A defense to an attempt

7. An inchoate offense

8. The requirement that a conspiracy involve at least two people

13. __ in the first degree is the individual who actually commits the crime

16. __ act test

Chapter 5

Justifications as Defenses

CHAPTER SUMMARY

I. Introduction

Study the Goetz case and understand why he did not qualify for the affirmative defense of self-defense.

II. Types of Defenses

A defense consists of evidence and arguments offered by a defendant to show why a person should not be held liable for a criminal charge. There are four types of defenses: alibi, inability of the prosecution to prove all of the necessary elements for conviction, justification, and excuses.

Justifications are based on the concept that the benefits of the conduct outweigh the harm or evil of the offense. An excuse is based on the concept that the actor should not be held legally responsible for his or her actions.

III. The Nature of Defenses

Justifications and excuses are affirmative defenses. Affirmative defenses must be asserted by the defendant are they are waived. Affirmative defenses do not negate any element of the crime, but rather build upon new matters which would excuse or justify the defendant's behavior. A successfully raised defense may have the effect of completely exonerating the defendant of any criminal liability.

IV. Justification as a Defense

Justifications include self-defense, defense of others, defense of home and property, consent, and resisting unlawful arrest.

A. Necessity

The concept of necessity forms the basis of all justifications. The defense of necessity claims that it was necessary to commit some unlawful act in order to prevent or to avoid a greater harm. The defense can only be claimed where the evil to be avoided is less than the harm caused.

B. Self-Defense

Self-defense is based on the recognition that a person has an inherent right to self-protection and that to reasonably defend oneself from an unlawful attack is a natural response to threatening situations. It may also be argued that one who acts in self-defense does not have the necessary state of mind to be convicted of a crime. The requirement that the use of force in self-defense be reasonable mandates that the accused behave as a reasonable person would under the same circumstances. The concept of a reasonable person envisions a person who acts with common sense and who has the mental capacity of an average, normal, sensible human being. Self-defense is also associated with the concept of apparent danger. Apparent danger exists when the conduct or activity of an attacker makes the threat of danger obvious.

The amount of force used in self-defense must also be reasonable. Reasonable force is that degree of force that is appropriate in a given situation and is not excessive. It is also the minimum degree of force necessary to protect oneself, one's property, a third person, or the property of another. Deadly force is considered as reasonable only when used to encounter an immediate threat of death or great bodily injury. Deadly force cannot be used against non-deadly force. Many jurisdictions impose the retreat rule before using deadly force. Generally there is no duty to retreat if an individual is at his or her home.

Some jurisdictions use the notion of perfect self-defense. Perfect self-defense is established when the evidence tends to show that at the time of the killing it appeared to the defendant, and he or she believed it to be necessary, to kill the defendant to save him or herself from imminent death or great bodily harm. An imperfect self-defense may exist where one or more of the conditions required for perfect self-defense are missing. An imperfect self-defense may lessen the degree of criminal liability.

C. Resisting Unlawful Arrest

Generally the use of resistance in the face of an unlawful arrest is considered as justifiable. Most jurisdictions provide statutory protections to law enforcement officers who find it necessary to use force to effect an arrest or to prevent persons who are in their custody from escaping.

The use of deadly force by law enforcement officers is of special concern. The deadly force may used only to prevent death or the threat of serious injury to the public, or to protect the law enforcement officer from a defendant who resorts to the use of deadly force.

D. Defense of Others

In the defense of others, some jurisdictions use the alter ego rule. This rule holds that a person can only defend a third party under circumstances and only to the degree that the third party could act. Other jurisdictions and the Model Penal Code allow a person to act in defense of another if the actor reasonably believes that his or her intervention is immediately necessary to protect the third person. Defense of others cannot be claimed by an individual who joins an illegal fight merely to assist a friend or family member. Force may also be used against a person to keep the person from hurting him or herself.

E. Defense of Home and Property

Defense of home and property can apply in the protection of personal property, defense of home, defense of another's property, and the use of a mechanical device to protect property. Generally the owner of property may use reasonable nondeadly force to prevent others from unlawfully taking or damaging his or her property. Deadly force is not permitted solely in defense of property. The setting of booby traps such as spring-loaded guns, electrified grates, explosive devices, and the like, is generally not permitted to protect property which is unattended and unoccupied.

The retreat rule generally does not apply to the protection of the home under the castle exception. The castle exception generally recognizes that a person has a fundamental right to be in his or her home, and also recognizes the home as a final and inviolable place of retreat. Property in the possession of a third person, or the home of a third person, may be protected by one who assists that person to the same degree and in the same manner that the owner of the property or the home would have been privileged to act.

F. Consent

The defense of consent makes the claim that the person suffering an injury either agreed to sustain the injury or that the possibility of injury in some activity was agreed to before that activity was undertaken. Consent is inherent in some situations. It must be voluntarily and legally given to be a valid defense. Sexual activity is an area where consent is frequently employed as a defense. Consent to one sexual act does not constitute consent to others. Understand the problems involved with implied consent and expressed consent. Consent cannot be claimed in the case of intimidation or fraud. Consent is not available as a defense in cases involving homicide or where the injury inflicted causes serious bodily harm.

CAPSTONE CASES: LEARNING ISSUES

United States v. *Thomas*

1.   Who has the burden of proof, prosecution or defense, to establish self-defense or the lack of self-defense?

2.   Why did the court determine that the defendants had no entitlement to any self-defense charge?

1. What specific conduct by defendant constituted reckless second-degree murder?

2. As a dog owner, what steps could the defendant have taken to prevent the crime?

3. Why was the state not required to prove that her dogs had vicious propensities of which she had knowledge?

PRACTICE TEST QUESTIONS

MULTIPLE CHOICE

___ 5.1. In the defense of ___, the defendant admits committing the act in question, but claims that it was necessary to avoid some greater harm.
a. excuse
b. justification
c. alibi
d. inability

___ 5.2. The _____ defense would be used when the defendant admits committing the act but claims that some personal condition or circumstance was such that he or she should not be held accountable under criminal law.
a. excuse
b. justification
c. alibi
d. inability

___ 5.3. In the defense of ___ the defendant claims he could not have committed the act because he or she was in a different location.
a. excuse
b. justification
c. alibi
d. inability

___ 5.4. Justifications and excuses are considered as ___ defenses.
a. passive
b. affirmative
c. negative
d. lack of capacity

___ 5.5. The concept of the ___ person envisions a person who acts with common sense and who has the mental capacity of an average, normal, sensible human being.

a. objective
b. ordinary
c. reasonable
d. subjective

___ 5.6.   The concept of ___ danger is associated with self-defense.
a. clear and present
b. present
c. apparent
d. real

___ 5.7.   The degree of force that is appropriate in a given situation and is not excessive is considered as ___ force.
a. deadly
b. ordinary
c. reasonable
d. subjective

___ 5.8.   _____ force is considered reasonable only when used to counter an immediate threat of death or great bodily harm.
a. Deadly
b. Ordinary
c. Reasonable
d. Subjective

___ 5.9.   Most jurisdictions impose a ___ rule on those who would claim self-defense.
a. subjective
b. non-deadly force
c. retreat
d. non-objective

___ 5.10.   Prior to the *Tennessee* v. *Garner* case, most law enforcement agencies used the _____ felon rule.
a. dangerous
b. reasonable
c. fleeing
d. objective

___ 5.11.   The defense of others is circumscribed by the ___ rule.
a. dangerous
b. reasonable
c. alter ego
d. subjective

___ 5.12. Generally speaking, ___ force is not permitted in defense of property.
a. deadly
b. non-deadly
c. reasonable
d. serious

___ 5.13. The ___ exception generally recognizes that a person has a right to be in his or her own home.
a. alter ego
b. retreat
c. dangerous
d. castle

___ 5.14. The defense of consent is generally only available in those offenses where ___ is an element of the crime.
a. non-consent
b. consent
c. serious bodily harm
d. personal injury

___ 5.15. The defense of consent may not be claim in cases involving
a. sexual conduct.
b. defense of property.
c. intimidation or fraud.
d. theft of personal property.

___ 5.16. An actor who was reckless in bringing about the situation may not use the ___ defense.
a. mistake
b. excuse
c. impossibility
d. justification

___ 5.17. An individual may use ___ force to protect his or her property.
a. deadly
b. reasonable
c. minor
d. subjective

___ 5.18. The highest degree of force is
a. deadly.
b. self-defense.
c. subjective.
d. objective.

____ 5.19   The degree of force that is appropriate for the situation and is not excessive is
             a. deadly.
             b. non-deadly.
             c. objective.
             d. reasonable.

____ 5.20.   Generally, the defense of ____ is not available to one who is the aggressor.
             a. necessity
             b. self-defense
             c. subjective

TRUE/FALSE

____ 5.21.   An affirmative defense consists of evidence and arguments offered by the prosecution to show why a person should be convicted of a crime.

____ 5.22.   Excuses are not considered as affirmative defenses.

____ 5.23.   An injury or damage is common to both excuse and justification defenses.

____ 5.24.   The defense of excuse is applicable where the individual finds himself or herself facing a choice between two evils and selects the "lesser evil."

____ 5.25.   Affirmative defenses attach the moral and legal authority of the state to bring a criminal charge against the defendant.

____ 5.26.   The concept of necessity forms the basis of all justifications.

____ 5.27.   It can be argued that one who acts in self-defense lacks the requisite mental element of the crime.

____ 5.28.   Deadly force may be used to protect valuable property.

____ 5.29.   In American jurisdictions, a person is never required to retreat before using deadly force in self-defense.

____ 5.30   Imperfect self-defense may be used to avoid prosecution.

KEY CONCEPTS

Identify the below key concepts from Chapter 5 of the text:

_____ 5.1.   A category of legal defenses in which the defendant admits committing the act in question but claims that it was necessary in order to avoid some greater evil.

_____ 5.2. A category of legal defenses in which the defendant claims that some personal conditions or circumstances at the time of the act was such that he or she should not be held accountable under criminal law.

_____ 5.3. That form of imminent danger that is said to exist when the conduct or activity of an attacker makes the threat of danger obvious.

_____ 5.4. Defenses that must be raised by the defendant independently of any claims made by the prosecutor, and include justifications and excuses.

_____ 5.5. A claim of self-defense that meets all of the generally accepted legal conditions for such claim to be valid.

_____ 5.6. Force likely to cause death or great bodily harm.

_____ 5.7. A degree of force that is appropriate in a given situation.

_____ 5.8. A defense based on the inherent right of self-protection.

_____ 5.9. A person who acts with common sense and who has the mental capacity of an average human being.

_____ 5.10. Verbally expressed willingness to engage in a specified activity.

FACTUAL SCENARIOS

1. Frank and Thomas meet on the campus one day. Frank attacks Thomas with a knife. Thomas reasonably believes that Frank is trying to kill him. Thomas could safely run away. Instead, he draws his pistol and kills Frank. Is Thomas criminally liable for Frank's death?

2. Jerry walks up to Jill, a former girlfriend, and tells her, "Tomorrow when I get my paycheck, I'm going to buy a gun and kill you." Jill immediately gets a gun out of her car and kills Jerry. Jill claims she killed in self-defense. Is this a valid self-defense?

3. Sue is attacked by a stranger. In self-defense, she throws a brick at the stranger. The brick accidentally hits a baby, injuring the baby. Is Sue guilty of a battery on the baby?

CROSSWORD 5

Across

3. Used to establish defenses

6. That form of danger that exists when the conduct or activity of an attacker makes the threat of danger obvious

8. He who ___ himself accuses himself.

11. A justification that claims that the injured party agreed to the injury or possibility of injury

13. The ___ rule is used in many jurisdictions as a requirement prior to using deadly force.

14. A person's home

15. A defense that claims it was required to commit the act in question to prevent a greater harm

16. Force that results in death or serious bodily injury

Down

1. Illegal

2. A category of legal defenses

3. Verbally indicated consent

4. Defending one's self

5. ___ felon rule

7. The ___ person standard

9. ___ self-defense

10. Subway shooter

12. ___ ego rule

13. ___ v. Dudley

Chapter 6

Excuses as Defenses

CHAPTER SUMMARY

I. Introduction

Read the Alice Mahaffey case and consider why voluntary intoxication is rarely a defense to criminal misconduct.

II. The Nature of Excuses

Excuses admit that the action committed by the defendant was wrong and that it violated the criminal law, but, claim that the defendant should be excused from criminal liability by virtue of special conditions or circumstances which suggest that the actor is not or was not responsible for his or her deeds. The majority of excuses are personal in nature. They claim that the defendant acted on the basis of some disability or some abnormal condition such as intoxication, insanity, or immaturity. Excuses are affirmative defenses.

III. Categories of Excuses

There are six generally accepted excuses which are discussed below. Understand the four conditions, according to Robinson, under which society is generally willing to excuse an actor.

A. Duress

The defense of duress, also referred to as compulsion, is based on the belief that people do not willfully engage in acts they are compelled or coerced to perform. In most jurisdictions, effective use of the duress defense must be based upon a showing that the defendant feared for his or her life, or was in danger of great bodily harm of another. Duress is generally available as a defense where the crime committed is less serious than the harm avoided. It is not a defense to criminal homicide. Some jurisdictions ban it as to all crimes of personal violence.

B. Intoxication

The law generally holds that a person who voluntarily puts himself in a condition so as to have little or no control over his actions must be held to have intended whatever consequences that may ensue. A claim of intoxication generally is not regarded as an effective defense even where the intoxication results from alcoholism. Involuntary intoxication generally results from the unknowing ingestion of an intoxicating substance. It may serve as a defense if it creates in the defendant an incapacity either to appreciate the criminality of one's conduct, or creates an incapacity to conform one's behavior to the requirements of the law.

C. Mistake

An honest mistake of fact will generally preclude criminal liability in instances where the actions undertaken would have been lawful had the situation been as the person acting reasonably believed it to be. An honest mistake is one which is genuine and sincere. An honest and reasonable mistake is one which is genuine and sincere and might be made by a typically competent person acting under the same set of circumstances. Mistake of fact refers to a lack of knowledge of some fact relating to the subject matter. It may refer to a misinterpretation or misunderstanding of the facts at hand.

A mistake of law is generally not a defense to criminal liability. In a few situations, mistake or ignorance of law may be a defense to an offense that requires specific intent. Ignorance of the law may be an excuse where the law is not adequately published, or is incapable of being known.

D. Age

Defenses based on age make the claim that persons should not be held criminally responsible for their activities by virtue of their youth. Under common law, children under the age of 7 were presumed to be without criminal capacity. Today in most states, children under the age of 7 cannot be charged with criminal offenses. Most jurisdictions do not impose full criminal culpability upon children under the age of 18. A number of states have lowered the age of responsibility to 16 or 17. Children under the age of criminal responsibility are subject to juvenile court jurisdiction. The defense of infancy is based on the chronological age of the defendant and not the mental maturity.

E. Entrapment

The defense of entrapment is based on the claim that were it not for government instigation, no crime would occur. The defense may be raised where public law enforcement officials or others acting on behalf of the government induce or encourage others to engage in illegal activity. The two most common inducements are false representation by officers that are calculated to induce the belief that the behavior in question is not illegal, and the use of inducements to crime that are so strong that a person of average will and good intent cannot resist.

Entrapment does not exist where the government merely provides an opportunity or facility for the commission of an offense. The subjective approach to gauging entrapment excludes from criminal liability persons otherwise innocent, who have been lured to the commission of the prohibited act through the government's instigation. This approach tries to distinguish between those who are blameworthy and those who are not, by asking whether a person caught by the government was predisposed to commit the crime in question. The subjective test looks at the origin of criminal intent.

The objective approach is based upon the belief that the methods employed on behalf of the government to bring about conviction cannot be countenanced. It is sometimes referred to as the defense of outrageous government conduct.

F. Syndrome-Based Defense Enhancements

Syndrome is a complex of signs and symptoms presenting a clinical picture of a disease or disorder. Syndromes are used to demonstrate that a person is suffering from a condition at the time that the crime was committed in an attempt to lower or eliminate criminal liability. The courts have been reluctant to recognize the claim that syndromes negate *mens rea*; the use of syndromes in expanding the applicability of traditional defenses has met with greater success. Syndromes are sometimes used to explain why a person committed the act in question in a particular situation. The most popular syndromes include Battered Women's Syndrome, Adopted Child Syndrome, False Memory Syndrome, Premenstrual Stress Syndrome, and Attention Deficit Disorder Syndrome.

CAPSTONE CASES: LEARNING ISSUES

State v. *Innis*

1. Explain the court's rationale when it stated that "the law does not require a woman exercise infallible judgment when she uses deadly force to repel her attacker if she has reasonable grounds to believe that she is in danger of suffering great bodily injury or losing her life?"

2. To determine whether deadly force was necessary, what questions, according to the court, should be considered?

3. Why did the court refuse to affirm the conviction?

Jacobson v. *United States*

1. What is the test for entrapment?

2. What facts did the court used to find that the defendant was not predisposed to commit the crime?

State v. *Day*

1. What facts did the defendant use to support his contention that he was the victim of an entrapment?

2. What constituted entrapment under the statute involved in this case [Section 7-12]?

PRACTICE TEST QUESTIONS

MULTIPLE CHOICE

___ 6.1. The defense of ____ is sometimes called "compulsion" and is based on the belief that people do not willfully engage in acts they are compelled to perform.
a. mistake
b. insanity
c. entrapment
d. duress

___ 6.2. Which of the below defenses cannot be used as a defense to criminal homicide?
a. mistake
b. insanity
c. self defense
d. duress

___ 6.3. If ____ intoxication creates in the defendant an incapacity either to appreciate the criminality of one's conduct, or creates an incapacity to conform one's behavior to the requirements of the law, it generally constitutes a defense to criminal conduct.
a. voluntary
b. involuntary
c. voluntary or involuntary
d. alcohol induced

___ 6.4. ____ intoxication is generally a defense only to the extent that it negates an element of an offense referred to by the phrase "with intent to" or "with an intention to."
a. Voluntary
b. Involuntary
c. Voluntary or involuntary
d. Alcohol induced

___ 6.5. A(n) ____ mistake means one which is genuine and sincere.
a. honest
b. factual
c. legal
d. objective

___ 6.6. A mistake of ___ is generally not an acceptable defense.
a. fact
b. law
c. identity
d. substance

___ 6.7. Mistake is a(n) ___ defense.
a. affirmative
b. passive
c. objective
d. subjective

___ 6.8. Joe has sexual intercourse with a dead woman, thinking that she was only asleep. He should use the mistake of ___ defense when charged with rape.
a. law
b. fact
c. fact and law
d. none of the above

___ 6.9. Under common law, children under the age of ___ years could not be charged with a crime.
a. six
b. seven
c. eight
d. ten

___ 6.10. Most jurisdictions do not impose full criminal culpability upon children under the age of ___ years.
a. 14
b. 15
c. 16
d. 18

___ 6.11. Juvenile defendants are not "found guilty"; instead they are adjudicated as
a. criminal.
b. delinquent.
c. abused.
d. juvenile offenders.

___ 6.12. The defense of infancy is based on the ___ age of the defendant.
a. mental
b. chronological
c. Both a and b
d. None of the above

___ 6.13.   The defense of ___ claims that the law enforcement agents manufactured the crime.
a. inducement
b. entrapment
c. duress
d. mistake

___ 6.14.   In the medical literature, a(n) ___ is a complex of signs and symptoms presenting a clinical picture of a disease or disorder.
a. syndrome
b. pathology
c. response
d. disease

___ 6.15.   Internet Addiction Disorder is considered as a(n) ___ based defense.
a. syndrome
b. pathology
c. response
d. enhancement

___ 6.16.   The defense of ___ has met with greater success in England than in the U. S.
a. PMS
b. IAD
c. BWS
d. UFO

___ 6.17.   Which of the below statements are correct regarding the defense of intoxication?
a. Intoxication is not a useful defense because most intoxicated individuals are responsible for their impaired state.
b. Involuntary intoxication is never a defense to criminal homicide.
c. Voluntary intoxication may be a defense to a general intent crime.
d. Voluntary intoxication caused by the taking of authorized medicine is generally a valid defense.

___ 6.18.   A mistake of ____ may be a valid defense to a criminal charge if made in good faith under circumstances involving a bona fide attempt to ascertain the meaning of the law through reliance on a public official.
a. fact
b. law
c. opinion
d. reason

___ 6.19.   The defense of infancy has not been successful when based on claims of ____ immaturity.
a. chronological

b. mental
c. physical
d. rational

____ 6.20.   The _____ approach to gauging entrapment attempts to distinguish between those who are blameworthy and those who are not, by asking whether the person was predisposed to commit the crime in quesiton.
a. objective
b. subjective
c. realistic
d. general

TRUE/FALSE

____ 6.21.   The majority of excuses used as defenses are personal in nature.

____ 6.22.   The essence of any defense based on intoxication can be found in the effect that an intoxicating substance has on the mental state of the defendant.

____ 6.23.   Voluntary intoxication generally results from the unknowing ingestion of an intoxicating substance.

____ 6.24.   Voluntary intoxication can also result from a biological condition under which a person's body ferments food.

____ 6.25.   A reasonable mistake is one that might be made by a typically competent person acting under the same set of circumstances.

____ 6.26.   Mistake of fact is different from ignorance of fact.

____ 6.27.   The infancy defense is based on the mental age of the offender.

____ 6.28.   At common law, children under the age of 6 years could be tried for some offenses.

____ 6.29.   The Battered Child's Syndrome is considered as an affirmative defense to child abuse.

____ 6.30.   Battered Woman's Syndrome is considered as a condition said to characterize women who live in abusive relationships.

KEY CONCEPTS

Identify the below key concepts from Chapter 6 of the text:

_____ 6.1.   The mistaken belief that if we identify a cause for conduct, including mental or physical disorders, then the conduct is necessarily excused.

_____ 6.2.   Complex of signs and symptoms presenting a clinical picture of a disease or disorder.

_____ 6.3.   Condition characterized by a history of repetitive spousal abuse and learned helplessness or the subjective inability to leave an abusive situation.

_____ 6.4.   Defense predicated on, or substantially enhanced by, the acceptability of syndrome-related claims.

_____ 6.5.   Lack of knowledge of the law or of the existence of a law relevant to a situation.

_____ 6.6.   An improper or illegal inducement to crime by agents of enforcement.

_____ 6.7   Child who violates the criminal law, or who commits a status offense.

_____ 6.8.   Lack of knowledge of some fact relating to the matter at hand.

_____ 6.9.   Defense that makes the claim that the offender should not be held criminally responsible for his or her criminal act by virtue of youth.

_____ 6.10. Misunderstanding or misinterpretation of the law relevant to the situation at hand.

FACTUAL SCENARIOS

1. The state has a statute that makes it a crime for anyone to willfully abandonment his or her spouse. David is charged with the abandonment of his pregnant wife. At trial, he testified that he did not know that his wife was pregnant at the time he left. In addition, he was not aware of the criminal law in question. What defense should he use? Should he be convicted?

2. Smith points a loaded pistol at Mary and threatens to kill her unless she kills Jake, her husband. Mary kills Jake and feels happy to be free of him. Is she guilty of criminal homicide?

3. Harold, while on a drunken binge, breaks into Mrs. Roman's house. She is not home, but has left a candle burning on the coffee table. As Harold enters the living room, he stumbles into the table and knocks over the candle. The candle starts a fire and burns the house down. Could Harold defend a criminal charge on the basis that had Mrs. Roman not left a burning candle the house would not have burned?

CROSSWORD 6

Across

1. ___ of fact may be a valid defense.

4. A condition where one is forced to act against one's will

5. Some claim they suffer from a ____ of the mind.

7. ____ error

10. A feeling of being compelled

12. A defense based on the conduct of the police

15. ____ intoxication

16. ___ ignorance

Down

2. ___ of the law is generally not a valid defense.

3. Spousal ____

6. Voluntary ____ is generally not a valid defense.

8. A defense based on age

9. An excuse-based defense

11. Battered person's ___

13. ___ Mahaffey

14. ___ Robinson

Chapter 7

The Defense of Insanity

CHAPTER SUMMARY

I. Introduction

The terms "insane" and "insanity" are legal, not medical, terms. The defense of insanity is an affirmative defense that can be subsumed under the category of excuses. There is a presumption of sanity and in the absence of evidence to the contrary an accused is assumed sane for all purposes.

II. Competency to Stand Trial

Competency to stand trial is a due process concern. It becomes an issue when a defendant is incapable of understanding the proceedings against him or her or is unable to assist in his or her own defense due to mental disease or defect. A person is competent to stand trial if the person, at trial time, has sufficient present ability to consult with his or her lawyer with a reasonable degree of understanding, and a rational as well as factual understanding of the proceedings against him or her. Competency to stand trial focuses on the defendant's condition at trial time, rather than at the time of the crime.

III. Purpose of the Insanity Defense

The insanity defense can impact criminal liability in two ways: (1) it may result in a finding that the *mens rea* required for a specific crime is lacking and therefore no crime was committed or, (2) it may lead to a showing that although the required state of mind was present at the time of the crime, the defendant should be excused from legal responsibility because of mental disease or defect.

IV. The Insanity Defense A Common Misunderstanding

A common misconception is that *mens rea* is automatically lacking in an insane defendant, and that the purpose of the insanity defense is to advance such a claim. The ability to distinguish between moral good and evil is a different issue than that of demonstrating a culpable *mens rea* when *mens rea* is understood as purposeful or intentional behavior. A person suffering from a mental illness may still act purposefully, even though they may not, due to mental disease, be able to fully appreciate the moral implications of their behavior.

V. What Is Insanity?

According to *Black's Law Dictionary*, "insanity" is the term used to denote that degree of mental illness which negates the individual's legal responsibility or capacity. It is a legal term, not a medical term. It does not refer to a particular mental condition recognized by psychiatrists. It is, however, predicated upon a disease or disability of the mind.

VI. History of the Insanity Defense

The insanity defense is based on the 1843 case of Daniel M'Naghten. This case formalized the two tests that had been used earlier and brought them together. The jury in that case was instructed: "The question to be determined is whether at the time the act in question was committed, the prisoner had or had not the use of his understanding, so as to know that he was doing a wrong or wicked act."

A. The *M'Naghten* Rule Knowing Right from Wrong

The *M'Naghten* case caused much public outcry and angered the Queen. To bolster traditional common law interpretations of insanity, the leadership of the House of Lords called judges from across the country to a special session. The *M'Naghten* Rule includes two possibilities: (1) a lack of *mens rea* (the person did not know what he was doing), and (2) an acceptable legal excuse (the person did not know that it was wrong).

B. Control Rules The Irresistible Impulse Test

The *M'Naghten* Rule focused only on the cognitive component of the personality and it did not allow for degrees of insanity. There was no middle ground. In the belief that some forms of behavior could not be controlled, the irresistible impulse test was developed. The irrestible impulse defense is that if at the time the crime was committed, a mental disease or disorder prevented the defendant from controlling his or her behavior. Some jurisdictions used the "policeman at the elbow" instruction to implement the test.

C. The *Durham* Rules Crime as a Product of Mental Disease

The U.S. Court of Appeals for the District of Columbia, concluding that the present tests for insanity were flawed, developed the *Durham* Rule. This rule, also known as the "product rule," is based on the belief that an inability to distinguish right from wrong is merely a symptom of mental disease, and that behavior resulting from the disease is a more apt determinant of legal insanity. The rule has been criticized because it fails to give the fact-finder any standard by which to measure the competency of the accused. The rule was rejected by the District of Columbia in 1972.

D. The ALI Test Substantial Capacity

The ALI substantial capacity test is a modernized version of the *M'Naghten* Rule, blended with control rules. It reads: "A person is not responsible for criminal conduct if at the time of such conduct as a result of mental disease or defect he lacks substantial capacity either to appreciate the criminality of his conduct or to conform his conduct to the requirements of the law."

E. Guilty But Mentally Ill (GBMI)

Ten states have adopted statutes which permit findings of guilty but mentally ill. The defendant may be found to have been mentally ill at the time that the crime was committed, and is not legally insane. This is equivalent to a finding of guilty and the court will sentence the defendant just as a person found guilty of the crime in question. It permits the jury to make an unambiguous statement about the factual guilt, mental condition, and moral responsibility of the defendant.

F. The Doctrine of Settled Insanity

For legal purposes, insanity is insanity regardless of its underlying cause. Mere addiction to narcotics or the compulsion to abuse alcohol does not excuse criminal behavior. If a person's abuse has resulted in a permanent mental disorder that meets the requirements of an insanity defense the individual may use the doctrine of "settled insanity" as defense to certain criminal conduct.

VII. Diminished Capacity

Diminished capacity is similar to the insanity defense in that it depends upon a showing that the defendant's mental state was impaired at the time of the crime. It is most useful where it can be shown that, because of some defect of reason or mental shortcoming, the defendant's capacity to form the required state of mind required by specific intent crimes was impaired. A diminished capacity defense is built upon the recognition that mental condition, though insufficient to exonerate, may be relevant to specific mental elements of certain crimes or degrees of crime. The Model Penal Code limits applicability of diminished capacity to cases in which capital punishment might be imposed. Some jurisdictions have eliminated the diminished capacity defense.

VIII. How Widely Used Is the Insanity Defense?

The insanity defense is not widely used. Most research studies indicate that it is used in less than 1% of the cases. Most of the time it is used in cases involving violent crimes and criminal homicides.

IX. Consequences of an Insanity Finding

Most defendants found not guilty by reasons of insanity are not released from custody. According to many reports, they are held on an average at least as long as persons found guilty and sent to prison. Most are confined in state mental hospitals. To continue to hold a person in civil commitment, the state must establish that the person poses a danger to self or others and requires continued confinement. Generally the individual has a right to hearings every six months or at least once a year, depending on state law.

X. Abolishing the Insanity Defense

Frustration over the inability of medical and legal professionals to agree on the nature of exculpatory insanity and the difficulties which attend the application of legal tests for insanity has led several states to abolish the insanity defense. Many claim that claims of insanity should only be considered at the sentencing phase of a criminal proceedings.

CAPSTONE CASES: LEARNING ISSUES

Miller v. *State*

1. Why was the defendant's medical history entered into evidence by both the defense and the prosecution?

2. What insanity test had been used in the State?

3. Did it matter to the court whether the defendant was permanently or temporarily insane at the act time? Why?

PRACTICE TEST QUESTIONS

MULTIPLE CHOICE

___ 7.1. Which of the below statements are correct regarding the issue of insanity?
a. A defendant who was insane at act time cannot be tried.
b. A defendant who was insane at act time is generally immune from criminal liability.
c. A defendant who is insane at trial time may be tried.
d. All of the above statements are correct.

___ 7.2. The terms "insane" and "insanity" are
a. medical terms.

b. psychiatric terms.

c. legal terms.

d. psychotic terms.

___ 7.3. A person is NOT competent to stand trial if the person

a. understands the legal significance of criminal conduct.

b. does not remember doing the criminal act in question.

c. lacks the present ability to consult with an attorney.

d. is a drug addict.

___ 7.4. Competency to stand trial focuses on the defendant's condition at the time of

a. the act.

b. arrest.

c. indictment.

d. trial.

___ 7.5. The federal test to determine whether a defendant is competent to stand trial is addressed in

a. *Dusky* v. *United States.*

b. *Durham* v. *United States.*

c. *Cooper* v. *Oklahoma.*

d. *M'Naghten* case.

___ 7.6. The U.S. Supreme Court, in ____, ruled that states must let criminal defendants avoid trials if it's more likely than not that they are incompetent.

a. *Dusky* v. *United States*

b. *Durham* v. *United States*

c. *Cooper* v. *Oklahoma*

d. *M'Naghten* case

___ 7.7. The ____ developed the "Knowing right from wrong" test.

a. *Dusky* v. *United States*

b. *Durham* v. *United States*

c. *Cooper* v. *Oklahoma*

d. *M'Naghten* case

___ 7.8. The existence of mental disease or disorder can also negate what element of a crime?

a. the act

b. the motive

c. *mens rea*

d. *actus rea*

___ 7.9.   Psychological or behavioral abnormalities associated with temporary or permanent dysfunction of the brain are referred to as
    a. associate disorders.
    b. dissociate disorders.
    c. organic mental disorders.
    d. schizophrenia.

___ 7.10.   Insanity can impact criminal liability in which of the below ways?
    a. It may result in a finding that the *mens rea* required is lacking.
    b. It may show that the defendant should be excused from legal responsibility.
    c. Both of the above answers are correct.
    d. All of the above answers are incorrect.

TRUE/FALSE

___ 7.11.   Insanity is a widely used defense in criminal homicide cases.

___ 7.12.   The defense of insanity is an affirmative defense.

___ 7.13.   If no evidence is submitted on the issue of sanity of an accused, the jury must find him or her not guilty.

___ 7.14.   A person who is insane cannot act purposefully.

___ 7.15.   Insanity is a legal, but not social, term.

___ 7.16.   Symptoms must exist for more than six months for a diagnosis of schizophrenia to be made.

___ 7.17.   The insanity defense had its modern roots in the United States.

___ 7.18.   The wrongfulness test has been at the center of controversy since its inception.

___ 7.19.   Most state penal codes contain some form of the wrongfulness test.

___ 7.20.   The ALI uses the product test.

KEY CONCEPTS

Identify the below key concepts from Chapter 7 of the text:

_____ 7.1.   Finding by the court that the defendant has sufficient present ability to consult with his or her lawyer with a reasonable degree of rational understanding and that he or she has a rational as well as factual understanding of the proceedings against him or her.

_____ 7.2. The fourth edition of the Diagnostic and Statistical Manual of Mental Disorders.

_____ 7.3. Plea of a defendant that he or she is not guilty of the offense charged because at the time the crime was committed, the defendant did not have the mental capacity to be held criminally responsibility for his or her actions.

_____ 7.4. Test for insanity that evaluates defense claims that, at the time the crime was committed, a mental disease or disorder prevented the defendant from controlling his or her behavior in keeping with the requirements of the law.

_____ 7.5. The product rule; holds that an accused is not criminally responsible if his or her unlawful act was the product of mental disease or mental defect.

_____ 7.6. Test holds that a person is not responsible for criminal conduct if at the time or such conduct as a result of mental disease or defects he or she lacks substantial capacity either to appreciate the wrongfulness of his or her conduct or to conform his or her conduct to the requirements of the law.

_____ 7.7. Rule for determining insanity that asks whether the defendant knew that what he was doing was wrong.

FACTUAL SCENARIOS

1. James, a college graduate with a degree in philosophy, is caught stealing a Rolex watch from the local jewelry store. At trial, James' counsel presented evidence that James was from a very wealthy family and that he already owned five Rolex watches. The defense also presented evidence that James was diagnosed as a kleptomaniac five years ago and that James could not resist the urge to own as many Rolex watches as possible. Under the *M'Naghten* test, may James be convicted of larceny? Using the M.P.C. approach, may he be convicted of larceny?

2. Phillip is arrested and charged with murder of his landlord. During jury selection, it becomes evident that Phillip does not remember anything that happened on the night that the landlord was murdered, nor does he understand the nature of the present legal proceedings. His counsel makes a motion to dismiss the jury and abate the proceedings because of Phillip's lack of mental capacity. You present evidence that for years Phillip has been on medication. While on medication, he is mentally alert. When he was arrested, his medication was taken away from him. The judge grants the defense motion and abates the trial. Two months later, the prosecution requests that the case be rescheduled for trial. Should the judge reschedule the trial? Does it matter that Phillip is unable to remember what happened on the night of the murder?

CROSSWORD 7

Across

3. ___ v. Oklahoma

6. The ___ capacity defense has been eliminated in California.

8. Diminished ___

11. A disorder characterized by apprehension, dread, and fear

13. The substantial capacity test

14. ___ Resources on the Worldwide Web

16. __ rule-crime as a product of mental disease

18. __ v. Louisiana

19. __ M'Naughten

Down

1. The rule that is also known as the Durham Rule

2. __ Hinckley

3. Mental state that indicates the ability to stand trial

4. United States v. ____

5. State of mind

7. A legal, not medical term

9. Lord Chief Justice

10. Guilty, but mentally ill

12. A disorder characterized by an inability to control impulses

15. A mental disorder associated with dysfunction of the brain

17. Affective disorder

20. Black's ___ Dictionary

Chapter 8

Legal and Social Dimensions of Personal Crime: Homicide

CHAPTER SUMMARY

I. Introduction

Read the Dalili case. What sentence would you have imposed if you were the judge in that cased.

II. Criminal Homicide

Not all homicides are criminal. Homicide is the killing of one human being by another human being. Justifiable homicides are those which are permitted under law. Excusable homicides are those that may involve some fault, but not enough for the act to be considered criminal. Criminal homicides refer to those homicides to which criminal liability may attach. At common law there were two types of criminal homicides, murder and manslaughter.

A. *Corpus Delicti*

The *corpus delicti* of a criminal homicide consists of the death of a human being and of the fact that the death was caused by a criminal act or agency of another person. Identity of the offender is not part of the *corpus delicti*. In most states to conduct a successful prosecution, the state must establish the *corpus delicti* of the crime. Discovery of the body of a murder victim, however, is not required.

B. Taking a Life

At common law, an essential element of criminal homicide was the "killing of a human being." By definition the victim must have been alive before the homicidal act occurred. The killing of a fetus was not chargeable as a criminal homicide unless the fetus was capable of living outside of the mother's body. In a few states, like California, the alive requirement has been modified to include the fetus. In some states illegal abortions may be charged as criminal homicides.

C. Defining "Death"

A central issue in criminal homicide cases is the definition of death. The Model Penal Code provides no definition of death. The common law rule was that death occurs when a

70

person's heartbeat and respiration cease. Brain death is used today by many courts to establish the death of the victim. Brain death is said to occur when a blood flow test, called a cerebral angiogram, or an EEG, produces no evidence of physiological or electrical brain activity for a period of time. Brain death can occur even though the victim's heart continues to beat, and respiration persists. Many jurisdictions have adopted the Uniform Determination of Death Act. This act provides that an individual who has sustained either (1) irreversible cessation of circulatory and respiratory functions, or (2) irreversible cessation of all functions of the entire brain, including the brain stem, is dead. More than 30 states have adopted a cessation of brain function approach to defining death.

D. Time of Death

Death may occur some time after the fatal injury. Criminal homicide prosecutions under common law required that the death of the victim occur within a year and a day from the time that the fatal act took place. The year and a day rule is still used in a few states. Some states, like California, have changed the length of time. In California, the death must occur within three years and a day after the fatal injury was inflicted. Other states have eliminated the rule.

E. Proximate Cause and Homicide

Criminal homicide must be the result of an affirmative act, an omission to act, or criminal negligence. The cause of death must not be so remote as to fail to constitute natural and probable consequences of the defendant's act. A determination of proximate cause requires that death be a natural and probable consequence of the act in question. Where concurring causes contribute to a victim's death, an accused may be held criminally liable by reason of his own conduct which directly contributes to the fatal results.

III. Murder

The elements of murder are (1) an unlawful killing, (2) of a human being, (3) with malice. First-degree murder includes any willful, deliberate, and premeditated killing. Premeditation means the act of deliberating or meditating upon, or planning, a course of action. In those states that have only two degrees of murder, all murders other than first-degree are second-degree murders.

A. Malice Aforethought

Malice refers to the intentional doing of a wrongful act without just cause or legal excuse. Malice encompasses the intentional carrying out of a hurtful act without cause, and hostility of one individual toward another. In criminal homicide cases, it means "intention to kill." Malice aforethought is a historical term which connotes a malicious design to kill or injure. It is essentially equivalent to premeditation. Presently, in American law it

71

includes several states of mind. Malice may be implied or expressed. Neither malice nor malice aforethought require an ill will or hatred toward the victim. Malice may exist where the killing is unpremeditated and may be inferred from surrounding circumstances.

B. Capital Murder

Capital murder refers to murders for which the death penalty is authorized. In some states, all murders in the first degree fall into the capital murder category. Generally, only persons who kill with clear intention, or who envision killing before the commission of their crimes are subject to the death penalty. Premeditated murder is murder in which the intent to kill is formed pursuant to preexisting reflection, rather than as the result of a sudden impulse or heat of passion. The true test of premeditation is not the duration of time available for thought, but rather the extent of reflection. In some jurisdictions, capital murder is also referred to as aggravated murder. Aggravated murder is murder with one or more aggravating circumstances.

C. Felony Murder

At common law, a defendant was guilty of murder if, while perpetrating a felony or attempted felony, another person died as a consequence of the crime, even if the death was not intentional. The felony-murder rule was abolished in England, but it is still retained in most U.S. jurisdictions. Generally, a death that results from the commission of an enumerated felony, i.e., rape, arson, robbery, or burglary constitutes first degree murder. The rule applies whether the defendant kills the victim intentionally, recklessly, negligently, accidentally, or unforeseeably.

IV. Manslaughter

Manslaughter is the unlawful killing of a human being without malice. The elements of manslaughter are (1) an unlawful killing, (2) of a human being, (3) without malice.

A. Voluntary Manslaughter

Voluntary manslaughter is the unlawful killing of a human being, without malice, which is done intentionally upon a sudden quarrel or in the heat of passion. Voluntary manslaughter would be murder except that it is committed in response to adequate provocation. Provocation is said to be adequate if it would cause a reasonable person to lose self-control. Sudden passion means passion directly caused by and rising out of provocation by the victim or of another person acting with the victim.

B. Involuntary Manslaughter

Involuntary manslaughter is an unlawful homicide that is unintentionally caused, and which is either (1) the result of an unlawful act other than a dangerous felony, or (2) which occurs as the result of criminal negligence or recklessness. The central difference between voluntary and involuntary manslaughter is that with involuntary manslaughter there is no intention to kill. An involuntary manslaughter conviction may be based on an accidental death caused by the defendant during the commission of an unlawful act that is not a dangerous felony. The conviction may also result from criminal negligence. Criminal negligence is negligence of such a nature and to such a degree that it is punishable as a crime. It is gross negligence.

V. Negligent Homicide

Negligent homicide does not exist in all jurisdictions. It may be defined as the killing of a person without the intent to kill, when the killing takes place while the offender is performing a negligent act, or when the offender fails to exercise reasonable, prudent care.

A. Vehicular Homicide

Some jurisdictions have the offense of vehicular homicide. Vehicular homicide is the killing of a human being by the operation of a motor vehicle by another in a reckless manner likely to cause the death of, or great bodily harm to, another.

VI. Suicide

At common law, suicide was murder and anyone who assisted another in committing suicide was a party to murder. The modern rule is that suicide is not murder because of the requirement that the killing be that of another individual. Many states have the crime of assisting a suicide.

CAPSTONE CASES: LEARNING ISSUES

State v. *Amado*

1. What was the dispositive issue in the case?

2. When is the right to claim self-defense forfeited?

3. What does the court by the term "bright line" rule when it states that self-defense is not available as a defense to a charge of felony murder?

Johnson v. *Texas*

    1.   Under the facts of this case, what test was used to determine whether the judge should instruct the jury on a lesser included offense?

    2.   What is the distinction noted by the court between murder, involuntary manslaughter, and criminally negligent homicide?

Maine v. *Michand*

    1.   What constitutes "adequate provocation?"

    2.   What are the limitations on the types of conduct deemed legally adequate to mitigate the punishment for a felonious homicide?

PRACTICE TEST QUESTIONS

MULTIPLE CHOICE

___ 8.1.   At common law, what were the two types of criminal homicide?
        a. first and second degree murder
        b. murder and negligent homicide
        c. voluntary and involuntary manslaughter
        d. murder and manslaughter

___ 8.2.   The term ____ refers only to those homicides to which criminal liability may attach.
        a. murder
        b. manslaughter
        c. criminal homicide
        d. negligent homicide

___ 8.3.   To successfully prosecute a person for criminal homicide, the state must establish the ____ of the crime.
        a. *stare decisis*
        b. location of the body
        c. *corpus delicti*
        d. All of the above.

___ 8.4.   Most states have adopted a cessation of ____ approach to defining death.
        a. heart beat
        b. respiration

c. brain function
d. psychological functions

____ 8.5.   At common law, death occurs when cessation of _____ occurs.
a. heart beat
b. respiration
c. brain function
d. psychological functions
e. Both a. and b. above

____ 8.6.   A victim is shot by the accused resulting in a non-fatal wound, but the victim dies on the operating table as a result of shock; the shooting will be considered to constitute the _____ cause of death.
a. concurring
b. contributing
c. proximate
d. indirect

____ 8.7.   First-degree murder includes any willful, deliberate, and _____ killing.
a. intentional
b. premeditated
c. wanton
d. reckless

____ 8.8.   The mental state which describes unjustifiable conduct which is extremely reckless is sometimes called
a. criminal negligence.
b. implied negligence.
c. depraved heart murder.
d. wanton murder.

____ 8.9.   Manslaughter differs from murder in that ___ and premeditation are lacking.
a. conduct
b. intent
c. motive
d. malice

____ 8.10.   The intentional and unlawful killing of a human without malice is generally considered
a. murder.
b. wanton murder.
c. involuntary manslaughter.
d. voluntary manslaughter.

___ 8.11. An unlawful homicide that is unintentionally caused and which occurs as the result of an unlawful act not amounting to a felony is a(n)
a. murder.
b. wanton murder.
c. involuntary manslaughter.
d. voluntary manslaughter.

___ 8.12. A non-criminal homicide that involves some fault is a(n)
a. justifiable homicide.
b. excusable homicide.
c. negligent homicide.
d. manslaughter.

___ 8.13. A state ordered execution is a(n)
a. justifiable homicide.
b. excusable homicide.
c. negligent homicide.
d. manslaughter.

___ 8.14. The "alive" requirement has been modified in some state where the unlawful killing of a fetus is now considered as a(n)
a. criminal homicide.
b. non-criminal homicide.
c. justifiable homicide.
d. excusable homicide.

___ 8.15. Negligence which is said to be "the want of ordinary care" is considered as
a. criminal negligence.
b. gross negligence.
c. ordinary negligence.
d. a wanton disregard for human life.

___ 8.16. Criminal negligence is generally regarded as a form of
a. neglect.
b. gross negligence.
c. ordinary negligence.
d. ordinary care.

___ 8.17. In some jurisdictions, deaths resulting from degrees of negligence below that required for manslaughter may give rise to prosecution for
a. negligent homicide.
b. non-negligent homicide.

c. involuntary manslaughter.
d. excusable homicide.

____ 8.18. While suicide is not a crime, ____ another to commit suicide is a crime.
a. aiding
b. advising
c. encouraging
d. Answers a., b., and c. are all correct.

____ 8.19. In many states, illegal abortion may be charged as
a. involuntary manslaughter.
b. murder.
c. a misdemeanor.
d. negligent homicide.

____ 8.20. Under common law, the death must occur within ____ from the time that the ultimately fatal act took place.
a. one year
b. one year and a day
c. three years
d. three years and a day

TRUE/FALSE

____ 8.21. Justifiable homicides are those homicides that involve some degree of fault, but not enough to be considered as criminal homicides.

____ 8.22. An accidental death and an accidental killing are interchangeable terms.

____ 8.23. At common law, there were only two types of criminal homicide: murder and manslaughter.

____ 8.24. All homicides are considered to be a violation of criminal law.

____ 8.25. To successfully prosecute, the state must find at least a portion of the body of the deceased.

____ 8.26. The blood flow test is one of the tests used to determine brain death.

____ 8.27. Only a few jurisdictions retain the "year and a day rule."

____ 8.28. Malice or intent to kill may be either expressed or implied.

___ 8.29. The most common statutory requirement for first degree murder is that the killing had been premeditated and deliberate.

___ 8.30. The maximum penalty for capital murder is death.

KEY CONCEPTS

Identify the below key concepts from Chapter 8 of the text:

_____ 8-1. Killing of a human being by the act, procurement, or omission of another human being.

_____ 8-2. Unlawful killing of a human being without malice.

_____ 8-3. Unlawful killing of a human being with malice.

_____ 8-4. Killing of a human being in a manner that the criminal law does not prohibit.

_____ 8-5. Death caused by unexpected or unintended means.

_____ 8-6. Conscious disregard of one's duties, resulting in injury, death, or damage to another.

_____ 8-7. A killing justified for the good of society, e.g. capital punishment.

_____ 8-8. Death determined by a "flat" reading on an EEG test.

_____ 8-9. Legislative model for determining death supported by the ABA and AMA.

_____ 8.10. Common law requirement that homicide prosecutions could not take place if the victim did not die within a year and a day from the time that the fatal act occurred.

_____ 8-11. Voluntary conscious conduct.

_____ 8-12. Any willful, deliberate, and premeditated unlawful killing.

_____ 8-13. Legal term that refers to the intentional doing of a wrongful act without cause or legal excuse.

_____ 8-14. Act of deliberating or mediating upon, or planning a course of action.

_____ 8-15. An unjustifiable, inexcusable, and unmitigated person-endangering state of mind.

FACTUAL SCENARIOS

1. Paul returned home early from a business trip and discovered his wife, Susan, in bed with Larry, his law partner. Paul went into a rage. He grabbed a knife and stabbed Larry. He then went into the kitchen and got a beer. As he watched a football game on television and drank his beer he became even more enraged. At half-time, he then went down to the local gun store and purchased a .38 caliber revolver. He then went home and after the game killed Susan. What crimes, if any, is he guilty of?

2. Tom, who lives in Miami, robbed the Commerce National Bank in Tampa. He drove away from the bank being careful not to attract attention by speeding. While returning to Miami he got into a wreck and killed a pedestrian. At the time he hit the pedestrian, he was looking at his rear-view mirror at a highway patrol that was following him. Had he been alert, he probably would have missed the pedestrian who was jay-walking. Is Tom guilty of murder under the felony-murder rule?

3. Frank is involved in an argument with Joe. Joe shoots him in the stomach. Frank is dying. He begs Paul to end his suffering. Paul shoots Frank in the head. Frank dies immediately from the head wound. May Paul be tried for murder?

4. This issue is commonly used in law school classes to discuss the crime of murder: Tom lives on the third floor of a high-rise apartment. He hears a noise and goes out on his balcony with his legally registered pistol. He looks up and sees a woman falling from the 20th floor. There is not doubt that she will suffer a horrible death when she hits the sidewalk below. To lessen her suffering, Tom takes his pistol and kills her before she hits the ground. Has Tom committed murder?

CROSSWORD 8

Across

1. ___ manslaughter

5. The unlawful killing of a human being without malice

7. A homicide that is permitted under the law

8. ___ v. Moan

10. The killing of a human being by the failure to exercise reasonable care

11. Negligence that reflects conscious disregard of one's duties

14. To be convicted of murder, your actions must be the ___ cause of the death.

17. Death determined by a flat reading on an EEG

18. ___ murder rule

19. A killing in a manner that criminal law does not prohibit

22. A legal term that refers to the intentional doing of a wrongful act without just cause or excuse

23. ____ provocation

Down

2. Uniform Determination of Death Act

3. The act of deliberating

4. The unlawful killing of a human being with malice

6. ___ v. Superior Court

9. Murder plus one or more aggravating factors

12. Not a crime in most states

13. A death penalty case

15. ___ delicti

16. Unjustifiable conduct that is extremely reckless

20. The year and a day rule pertains to the ___ of death

21. An unborn child

Chapter 9

Legal and Social Dimensions of Personal Crime: Assault, Battery, and Other Personal Crimes

CHAPTER SUMMARY

I. Introduction

This chapter discusses personal crimes except for homicide.

II. Assault, Battery, and Mayhem

There is considerable overlap between the crimes of assault, battery, and mayhem. While assault and battery are often used as interchangeable, they are different and distinct crimes. An assault is either an attempted battery or a threatened battery. A battery is a consummated assault. Some state codes use attempted battery in lieu of an assault. Mayhem is a battery that causes great bodily harm or disfigurement.

A. Assault

The two common law crimes of assault were the attempted battery and the threatened battery. An attempted-battery-type assault occurs when an offender attempts to commit a battery on another person. The threatened-battery-type assault occurs when a victim is placed in fear of imminent injury. Some states, like California, does not recognize the threatened-battery-type assault. The elements of the attempted-battery-type assault are: an unlawful attempt, with present ability, to commit a battery.

Any attempt to commit an injury or an offensive touching must be unlawful. Thus, the use of force by law enforcement officers in a legal arrest is not an unlawful attempt to commit a battery. The present ability element of assault requires that the act that is attempted is physically capable of being carried out by the defendant, and that the method he or she intends to or threatens to use will in fact inflict an injury or offensive touching if carried out. It does not, in most jurisdictions, refer to the fact that for some reason or condition unknown to and not controlled by the defendant, the intended injury cannot actually be inflicted.

Bodily injury has a special meaning in assault and battery crimes. It does not mean that the injury attempted must be a severe one or cause great physical pain. The mere unlawful application of physical force on the person of another is sufficient. The terms "violence" and "force" are synonymous and include any application of force even though it entails no pain or bodily harm, and leaves no mark.

B. Placing Another in Fear

The threatened-battery-type assault requires that the defendant intends to create fear of imminent injury to the victim. In some jurisdictions it is described as "intentional-frightening assault." Words alone will not suffice, and some overt act must occur before the crime is committed.

C. Conditional Assaults

An assault may be committed where the danger or threat is conditioned upon a meeting of the assailant's demands. To constitute an assault, the condition must be one that the defendant is not entitled to place on the victim.

D. Aggravated Assaults

A simple assault is an assault without any aggravating circumstances. Aggravated assaults are generally assaults with intent to commit some other offense, such as rape or murder. Aggravated assaults also include special category assaults such as assault with a deadly weapon or assault on a peace officer.

E. Attempted Assaults

The law pertaining to criminal attempts generally does not apply to assaults. A few courts have created the crime of attempted assault. In these cases, the courts are referring to situations where efforts to accomplish battery had proceeded beyond the preparation stage, but not far enough to constitute an assault.

F. Anti-Stalking Statutes

The strict requirements of criminal assault crimes have lead many to believe that traditional criminal laws are not adequate to encompass the conduct of stalkers. One problem with the stalking statutes is the constitutional prohibition against vague statutes.

G. Battery

Battery is the causing of bodily injury or the offensive touching of another. The elements of battery are (1) the willful and unlawful, (2) use of force, violence, or offensive contact, (3) against the person of another. Any unjustified offensive touching constitutes a battery. The law against battery demands respect for the integrity of one's personal space. While battery is considered as an intentional crime, in most jurisdictions it may be committed recklessly or with criminal negligence. The doctrine of transferred intent provides that if an assailant intends to injure one person and by mistake injures another, he or she is guilty of battery. In some cases, a constructive touching is sufficient to constitute battery. For example the hitting of a horse that a person is riding may constitute battery.

Sexual battery occurs when a person unlawfully touches an inmate part of another person's body against that person's will and for the purposes of sexual arousal, gratification, or abuse. Sexual battery may also include cases of forced intimate touching where the victim is institutionalized for medical treatment and is seriously disabled or medically incapacitated. Many state statutes and the Model Penal Code define assault to include both assaults and batteries.

H. Aggravated Battery

Aggravated battery is a statutorily created crime that did not exist at common law. Like aggravated assault, aggravated battery may involve the use of a dangerous weapon, acts committed with the intention of committing another crime (e.g., rape or murder), or cases of battery that result in serious injury.

I. Mayhem

Common law did not recognize aggravated forms of assault and battery. The crime of mayhem was developed as an alternative. To constitute mayhem, the injury suffered by the victim had to be serious and permanent. At early common law, the injury must have been one that lessened the ability of the victim to defend him- or herself. Later mayhem was broadened to include injuries that are disfiguring. The elements of the crime of mayhem are (1) an unlawful battery, involving, (2) maliciously inflicting or attempting to inflict violent injury, and (3) one or more disabling or disfiguring injuries resulting from the battery.

III. Sex Offenses

The attitudes about sexual relationships are highly controversial and are themselves in a state of flux. Most people agree that unwanted and nonconsensual sexual activity should be subject to criminal prosecution, and that sex with a child under the age of legal consent should be criminalized. Criminal sexual conduct is a gender-neutral term and is applied today to a wide variety of sex offenses.

A. Rape

At common law, the crime of rape was the carnal knowledge of a woman forcibly and against her will. Carnal knowledge meant sexual intercourse. At common law any sexual penetration of the female vagina by the male penis was sufficient to complete the crime of rape. Penetration of the anus or mouth was referred to as deviate sexual intercourse. A husband could not rape his wife at common law. This has been changed in some jurisdictions. Other jurisdictions have the crime of spousal rape. The elements of the crime of rape are (1) sexual intercourse with a person not the spouse of the perpetrator, (2) through force, threat of force, or by guile, and (3) without the lawful consent of the victim.

Forcible rape is nonconsensual sexual intercourse which is accomplished against a person's will by means of force, violence, duress, menace, or fear of immediate and unlawful bodily injury to the victim. Most jurisdictions require that the unlawful intercourse must be committed by force, fraud, or forcible compulsion, except in those situations where the victim is unable to give legal consent. The central element in the definition of rape is the absence of the female's consent. First degree rape in many jurisdictions is rape committed by an armed offender, rape resulting in serious bodily injury to the victim, or gang rape.

Lawful consent may be lacking during sexual intercourse under any number of circumstances. If the victim is unable to give legal consent, then the intercourse will be rape. Lack of consent can be established by any acts of the victim that would lead a reasonable person to believe that he or she does not consent to the intercourse.

Statutory rape did not exist at common law. It has been enacted by statute in all American jurisdictions. In most jurisdictions, it is a strict liability crime. Statutory rape is having sexual intercourse with a child below a certain specified age.

B. Same-Sex Rape

Rape at common law required both penetration and an unwilling female victim. Today in many jurisdictions the rape statutes are gender-neutral. In other jurisdictions homosexual rape is considered as a sexual battery.

C. Rape Shield Laws

Rape shield laws are designed to protect victims of rape. A rape shield law generally provides that the relevancy of any evidence regarding the past sexual conduct of a rape victim must be demonstrated before it can be presented in court. The laws concern themselves more with appropriate courtroom procedure than they do with criminal behavior.

D. Sexual Assault

A recent trend is to combine all nonconsensual sexual offenses into one crime called sexual assault. Sexual assault encompasses far more than the common law crime of rape. It generally includes deviate sexual intercourse, fellatio, and statutory rape.

IV. Kidnapping and False Imprisonment

Kidnapping and false imprisonment are crimes that intimately invade a person's privacy and take away his or her liberty, often in abrupt and forceful fashion.

A. Kidnapping

Kidnapping is the unlawful removal of a person from the place where he or she is found, against the person's will, and through the use of force, fraud, threats, or some other form of intimidation. Most jurisdictions hold that any unlawful movement of the victim that is substantial is sufficient to satisfy the movement (asportation) requirement. The primary issue is whether the person is forcefully moved against his or her will, and not the degree of movement or distance involved. The elements of the kidnapping are (1) an unlawful taking and carrying away, (2) of a human being, (3) by force, fraud, threat, or intimidation, and (4) against the person's will. Kidnapping for ransom is considered as aggravated kidnapping.

Federal kidnapping law, the Lindbergh Law, was created in response to the kidnapping of the infant son of Charles A. Lindbergh. Other federal laws make it a crime to take a hostage, or to knowingly receive, possess, or dispose of any money or property that has been delivered as ransom on behalf of a victim of kidnapping.

B. False Imprisonment

False imprisonment is the unlawful violation of the personal liberty of another. It is similar to kidnapping except that it does not involve the carrying away of the victim. The elements of false imprisonment are (1) an unlawful restraint by one person, (2) of another person's freedom of movement, and (3) without the victim's consent or without legal justification.

V. Terrorism

A. Terrorism and the Law

Terrorism is a crime under federal law and now most states have enacted statutes making it a state crime. The problem is defining "terrorism." A rape victim is certainly involved in a terrorizing incident, but it does not meet the general statutory definition of a crime of terrorism. The most generally accepted definition of the crime is in the Foreign Relations Authorization Act discussed in Chapter 9 of the text. That definition is: "premeditated, politically, motivated violence perpetrated against non-combatant targets by sub-national groups or clandestine agents.

B. The USA Patriot Act

The Patriot Act was passed in response to the terrorist attacks of September 11, 2001. There have been serious criticisms regarding whether or not the Act violates certain constitutional rights designed to protect the rights of individuals. The act is due to expire at the end of 2005. Congress is presently considering whether to extend it, modify it, or allow it to expire.

CAPSTONE CASES: LEARNING ISSUES

In re John Z

    1.   What was the conflict in the court of appeals decisions that the court was concerned with?

    2.   When should a woman have the right to withdraw consent to sexual intercourse?

    3.   What did the court mean when it disapproved "Vela to the extent that decision is inconsistent with our opinion?"

Clark v. *Carey*

    1. What affect did the Antiterrorism and Effective Death Penalty Act have on this case?

    2. What test does the court use in determining whether the evidence is sufficient to support the finding of guilty?

    3. What was the issue regarding the movement of the bank manager from the outside to the inside of the bank?

Schweinle v. *State*

    1.   Why did the court decide the case only on one of four issues and never discussed the other issues?

    2.   Why was it important to determine whether the evidence raised the issue of the lesser included offense of false imprison?

Clements v. *State*

    1.   Under what grounds did the defendant argue that the stalking statute was unconstitutional?

    2.   What is meant by a "legal sufficiency review?"

PRACTICE TEST QUESTIONS

MULTIPLE CHOICE

____ 9.1.   To constitute an assault, any attempted injury or offensive touching must be
    a. with consent.
    b. without intent.
    c. unlawful.
    d. authorized.

____ 9.2.   The two types of assault at common law are the attempted battery and the
    a. attempted assault.
    b. conditioned assault.
    c. conditioned battery.
    d. threatened battery.

____ 9.3.   An assault with the intent to commit murder is a(n)
    a. battery.
    b. felony battery.
    c. aggravated assault.
    d. aggravated battery.

____ 9.4.   A major difference between attempt and assault is that an accused may be convicted of a(n) ____ even if consummation of the primary offense is impossible to complete.
    a. attempt
    b. assault
    c. battery
    d. aggravated assault

____ 9.5.   The offense of battery occurs when a person
    a. actually and intentionally touches another person against the will of the other.
    b. actually and intentionally strikes another person against the will of the other.
    c. intentionally causes harm to another person.
    d. All of the above statements are correct.
    e. Only statements b. and c. are correct.

____ 9.6.   The doctrine of transferred intent applies to the crime of
    a. simple assault.
    b. aggravated assault.

c. battery.
d. none of the above crimes

___ 9.7. Touching that is implied by law to replace the actual touching requirement is referred to as
a. transferred touching.
b. implied touching.
c. constructive touching.
d. expressed touching.

___ 9.8. An accused who commits an unlawful battery involving the malicious infliction of a serious injury that results in the loss of the victim's limb may be prosecuted for which of the below listed crimes?
a. aggravated assault
b. aggravated battery
c. mayhem
d. The accused may be prosecuted for any of the above listed crimes.

___ 9.9. The term "carnal knowledge" refers to
a. the unlawful touching of a female.
b. sodomy.
c. criminal sexual conduct with a child.
d. sexual intercourse.

___ 9.10. Consensual sex with a 12-year-old female by a 21-year-old male constitutes the crime of
a. sodomy.
b. incest.
c. rape.
d. carnal knowledge.

___ 9.11. The term ____ refers to the oral stimulation of the male penis.
a. fellatio
b. sodomy
c. statutory rape
d. spousal rape

___ 9.12. False imprisonment is a lesser and included offense to the crime of
a. aggravated battery.
b. kidnapping.
c. mayhem.
d. sexual assault.

___ 9.13. The unlawful movement of a person from one county to another against that person's will and through the use of force constitutes the crime of
a. false imprisonment.
b. kidnapping.
c. aggravated assault.
d. aggravated battery.

___ 9.14. Most states classify the crime of false imprisonment as a(n)
a. infraction.
b. felony.
c. misdemeanor.
d. capital offense.

___ 9.15. The arrest of a person without lawful authority constitutes the crime of
a. kidnapping.
b. false imprisonment.
c. false arrest.
d. Both b. and c. are correct.

___ 9.16. The basic difference between the crimes false imprisonment and kidnapping is that false imprisonment does not involve
a. a restraint of the personal liberty of the victim.
b. the element of consent.
c. the carrying away of the victim.
d. legal justification.

___ 9.17. The present ability element of ___ requires that the act that is attempt is physically capable of being carried out by the accused.
a. assault
b. battery
c. mayhem
d. stalking

___ 9.18. The recent trend regarding sexual offenses is to combine all ___ sexual offenses into the crime of sexual assault.
a. consensual
b. nonconsenual
c. violent
d. non-violent

___ 9.19. Which of the below offenses is considered as a first degree rape?
a. gang rape
b. statutory rape

      c. spousal rape

      d. sodomy

___ 9.20.   Anti-stalking statutes generally require a(n) ____ threat to constitute the offense.

      a. aggravated

      b. credible

      c. dangerous

      d. verbal

TRUE/FALSE

___ 9.21.   An assault with a dangerous weapon may be committed with a weapon that is not dangerous *per se*.

___ 9.22.   One of the problems with anti-stalking statutes is the constitutional provision against vagueness.

___ 9.23.   Sexual battery requires that the touching be for the purposes of sexual arousal, gratification, or sexual abuse.

___ 9.24.   The accused's reasonable belief that the victim effectively consented to sexual intercourse is not a defense to rape.

___ 9.25.   Rape at common law required that an emission occur.

___ 9.26.   The purpose of rape shield laws are designed to ensure that the accused receives a fair trial.

___ 9.27.   The first anti-stalking statute was passed in California.

___ 9.28.   Kidnapping under modern statutes requires that the victim be moved from one county to another.

___ 9.29.   False imprisonment is a violation of the personal liberty of the victim.

___ 9.30.   Kidnapping for ranson is an aggravated form of kidnapping.

KEY CONCEPTS

Identify the below key concepts from Chapter 9 of the text:

_____ 9.1.   The rape of one's spouse.

_____ 9.2. The unlawful touching of an intimate part of another person against that person's will and for the purposes of sexual arousal, gratification, or abuse.

_____ 9.3. Intentionally removal of an ear of a victim.

_____ 9.4. A gender neutral term that is applied to a wide variety of sex offenses.

_____ 9.5. Oral or anal copulation between persons of the same or different gender, or between a human being and an animal.

_____ 9.6. An intentional and offensive touching of the person of another.

_____ 9.7. Any contact between any part of the genitals of one person and the mouth or anus of another.

_____ 9.8. Attempted battery.

_____ 9.9. The unlawful application of physical force on the person of the victim-even where no physical harm results.

_____ 9.10. Assault with the intent to commit murder.

_____ 9.11. The intentional frightening of another through following, harassing, annoying, tormenting, or terrorizing activities.

_____ 9.12. A touching that is inferred or implied from prevailing circumstances.

_____ 9.13. Legal consent.

FACTUAL SCENARIOS

1. Bill Gates, a multimillionaire, is traveling in Texas. Two college students, who are unhappy because they cannot get a job in the computer industry, plan to hit Gates in the face with a pie. As Gates gets off his airplane in Dallas, the two students run up to him and attempt to hit him in the face with the pie. They miss him and hit his wife. What crimes, if any, have they committed?

2. Paul met Linda in a local bar. When they met, it was obvious to Paul that Linda had had too many drinks. He then asked her if she would like to go to his apartment and sleep in his spare bedroom. When they arrived at his apartment, he took her into his bedroom and undressed her. Then he began to have sex with her. During the sex, Linda laughed and did not resist. When Linda got up the next day, she went to the police and charged Paul with rape. At trial, Linda testified that had she not been intoxicated, she would not have consented to the sexual act. It was also

established that Paul should have known that Linda was incapable of consenting to the sexual act. Paul takes the stand and testifies that he honestly believed that she consented to the sexual act. Paul's counsel attempts to enter into evidence that Linda had been arrested five years ago for prostitution. Should Linda's police record be admitted into evidence? May Paul be convicted of rape? Would your answer be different if Paul had gotten Linda intoxicated?

CROSSWORD 9

Across

1. "If you do not move, I will hit you" is a ____ assault.

7. Intent imposed by law

10. A threatened battery

11. Permission

12. Legal consent

15. Sexual battery is an ____ assault.

16. Oral stimulation of the penis

Down

1. ____ touching

2. Rape that is accomplished by means of violence

3. False imprisonment plus substantial movement of the victim

4. ____ rape is a statutory crime in many states.

5. Rape of a minor

6. Unlawful physical violence inflicted upon another individual with his or her consent

8. Rape ____ laws

9. The intentional frightening of another through following, harassing, annoying, tormenting, or terrorizing activities

13. By ____ or threat of force against another person

14. Sexual intercourse without legal consent

Chapter 10

Legal and Social Dimensions of Property and Computer Crimes

CHAPTER SUMMARY

I. Introduction

Why could Sadie Daniels be convicted of theft?

II. Theft Crimes

Most property crimes are crimes of theft. Theft is a general term embracing a wide variety of misconduct by which a person is improperly deprived of his or her property. The purpose of theft law is to promote security of property by threatening aggressors with punishment. Theft crimes are sometimes called acquisitive offenses, wrongful acquisition crimes, or crimes of misappropriation.

At early common law, only larceny was a crime. Larceny is the wrongful taking and carrying away by any person of the mere personal goods of another, from any place, with a felonious intent to convert them to his or her own use. Only personal property was subject to larceny. Outright cheating and misappropriation of goods entrusted into the care of another were not regarded as crimes. As commerce grew, common law expanded to punish new forms of theft. The crimes of embezzlement, extortion, and obtaining property by false pretenses developed. The modern trend in most jurisdictions is to merge all acquisitive crimes into one theft crime.

A. Larceny

Larceny was the first and most basic property crime at common law. Larceny is the wrongful taking of personal property from the possession of another. Larceny is a crime against possession, not ownership, since the person from whom the item was stolen could still be said to have ownership even if he or she was no longer in possession of the property.

Larceny is (1) trespassory taking, (2) carrying away (asportation) of, (3) the personal property of another, (4) with the intent to steal. Larceny is either petty or grand. Grand larceny is the stealing of property that has a market value in excess of a certain specified amount, or the theft of certain statutorily listed property, such as firearms and cattle. All other thefts are petty thefts.

At common law only tangible personal property could be subject to the crime of larceny. Tangible property is property that has a physical form. Personal property is anything of value that is subject to ownership that is not land or fixtures. The property must have some value, however slight.

At common law there could be no larceny unless there were a trespassory taking. The taking generally consists of a physical seizure by which one exercises dominion and control over the property. A trespassory taking is merely a taking without the consent of the victim.

The breaking the bulk doctrine developed from the English case known as the "Carrier Case." Under this doctrine, the owner was considered to retain constructive possession of the goods in transit and the breaking of the bulk by the carrier was considered as a trespassory taking of the goods.

To constitute larceny, there must be a carrying away of the property. This is called asportation. Even the slightest movement, if done in a carrying away manner, is sufficient to constitute asportation. In some jurisdictions, the asportation requirement is viewed merely as a means of assuring that the defendant had dominion and control over the property.

The property must belong to the person of another. A person cannot be convicted of larceny if he or she owns the property and has a right to possession of it. In some jurisdictions, it is larceny to steal your own property if someone else has a greater right to possession of the property.

Larceny is a specific intent crime. It cannot be committed negligently nor recklessly. The intent to steal requirement means that the offender intends to wrongfully deprive one who lawfully has possession of an item.

B. Embezzlement

Larceny requires a trespassory taking. Embezzlement is the wrongful appropriation of property that has been entrusted to the offender. The central feature of embezzlement is the wrongful conversion of property. Embezzlement involves a breach of trust. Research on embezzlement cases shows that employees who embezzle tend to have higher levels of indebtedness, change jobs more frequently, and have lower incomes than employees in similar positions with other companies.

C. False Pretenses

The crime of obtaining property by false pretenses is a form of theft which also involves transfer of ownership or title. Contrary to embezzlement, the transfer of ownership or the passing of title is obtained by an unlawful and false representation. It is the knowingly and unlawfully obtaining title to, and possession of, the lawful property of another by means of deception, and with intent to defraud. The false representation must be material.

D. Forgery

Forgery is the making of a false instrument or the material alteration of an existing genuine written instrument. Forgery is complete when the perpetrator either makes or passes a false instrument with the intent to defraud. The gist of the crime is the intent to defraud, not the act of defrauding. The act of uttering a forged document is the offering, passing, or attempting to pass a forged document with knowledge that the document is forged. The elements of forgery are (1) a false signature or material alteration, (2) signed or altered without authority, (3) of a writing or other instrument that, if genuine, would have legal significance, and (4) with intent to defraud. The elements of uttering a forged document are (1) possession or creation of a forged document that, if genuine, would have legal significance, (2) the uttering, passing, publishing, or attempting to pass the forged document, and (3) with the intent to defraud.

E. Receiving Stolen Property

Receiving stolen property is the knowingly taking possession of or control over property that has been stolen from another. It is the receiving of stolen property, knowing that it was stolen. Receiving for purposes of this crime means acquiring control over, taking possession of, or taking title to, any property. The elements of the crime are (1) receiving, (2) stolen property, (3) which the receiver knew was stolen, and (4) where the property was received with the intent to deprive the rightful owner of its possession.

F. Robbery

Robbery is a violent, personal crime. The object of robbery is the unlawful acquisition of property. Robbery is the unlawful taking of property that is in the immediate possession of another by force or threat of force. Robbery is an aggravated form of larceny. The elements of robbery are (1) the felonious taking of personal property, (2) from the person or immediate presence of another, (3) against the will of the victim, and (4) accomplished by means of force or by putting the victim in fear.

G. Extortion

At early common law, extortion was the corrupt collection of an unlawful fee by a public officer under color of office, or the attempt to collect such a fee. The crime has been expanded to include all persons using the threat of future actions to wrongfully obtain property or services. Extortion differs from the crime of robbery in that robbery occurs when property is taken by force or threat of immediate violence. In extortion the defendant obtains property by threat of future violence. Blackmail is a form of extortion in which a threat is made to disclose a crime or other social disgrace. Extortion differs from compounding a crime, which consists of the receipt of property or other valuable consideration in exchange for an agreement to conceal or not prosecute one who has committed a crime. Compounding a crime involves a mutual agreement between parties, whereas extortion is based on a qualified threat.

H. Identity Theft

Identity theft is now one of the most important new theft crimes. Note how it differs from other types of theft.

III. Consolidation of Theft Crimes

To reduce the complexities that surround theft crimes, many jurisdictions have consolidated the theft crimes into the single crime of theft. Such laws combine two or more of the common law crimes of larceny, embezzlement, extortion, receiving stolen property, and false pretenses into the crime of theft.

IV. Burglary

At common law, burglary was the breaking and entering the dwelling house of another at night with intent to commit a felony. In most states, the crime of burglary is statutorily defined as the (1) breaking and (2) entering of (3) a building, locked automobile, boat, etc. (4) with the intent to commit a felony or theft. Generally, first degree burglary is the burglary of an inhabited dwelling. Other burglaries are generally of second degree burglary.

The breaking requirement does not necessitate any damage to the property burglarized, although it is usually interpreted as requiring the use of actual or constructive force to create an opening in the thing being burglarized. The forced opening of any part of a structure is sufficient. The obtaining entry by fraud, threatening to use force against another person, and by having a co-conspirator open a door from within have been held sufficient to constitute constructive breaking.

The breaking must be trespassory. Generally a defendant who enters with permission is not guilty of burglary. Consent is not effective if given by a person the defendant knows is not legally authorized to provide it. In addition to breaking, actual or constructive entry is required. The slightest intrusion by the burglar or by any part of the burglar's body into the structure is sufficient. A constructive entry is when the defendant causes another person to enter the structure to commit the crime or achieve the felonious purpose. There must be a casual relationship between the breaking and the entry.

Criminal trespass is a lesser included offense of burglary. Criminal trespass is the entering or remaining on the property or in the building of another when entry is forbidden, or failing to depart upon having received notice to do so. Criminal mischief is the intentional or knowing damage or destruction of the tangible property of another. Looting is burglary committed within an affected geographical area during an officially declared state of emergency, or during a local emergency caused by a natural or manmade disaster.

V. Arson

At common law, arson was the malicious burning of the dwelling of another. The crime was committed against habitation, not against property. The punishment was death by burning. Generally arson has been expanded to include many items other than structures and the crime is now considered as a crime against property. Arson requires the knowing and malicious burning of the fixture or personal property of another. Arson cannot be committed by negligent or reckless conduct. Most jurisdictions have the crimes of recklessly starting a fire and unlawfully causing a crime. Arson occurs with the slightest malicious burning of the property. A discoloration or blackening by heat or smoke is not regarded as sufficient to constitute a burning.

VI. Computer and High-Technology Crimes

Crimes which employ computer technology as central to their commission, and which could not be committed without it, are considered as computer crimes. Because computer crimes generally violate traditional laws as well as laws specifically designed to combat computer crimes, many prosecutors successfully prosecuted early computer crimes under embezzlement, larceny, and fraud statutes.

A. Early Computer Crime Cases

Although some of the early defendants in the computer crime area were able to avoid criminal liability by playing on the shortcomings of traditional statutes defining property crimes, most were not. Most courts and prosecutors had little difficulty applying traditional concepts to computer crimes. Federal prosecutors used wire fraud and mail fraud charges where state prosecutors would have charged fraud, larceny, or embezzlement.

B. Computer Crime Laws

All fifty states and the federal government have enacted computer crime statutes. The first state was Florida and the last one was Massachusetts. The first federal statute was the Computer Fraud and Abuse Act enacted in October, 1984. Central to the federal statutes is the provision which makes it a federal crime to access, without authorization, any data processing system if the data processing system is involved in or used in relationship to interstate commerce. The concept of a federal interest computer was also developed.

C. Types of Computer Crimes

The contemporary term for computer crime is cybercrime. Cybercrime is crime committed with or through the use of computers. There are five types of cybercrime found in today's law. The five types are: (1) computer fraud, (2) computer trespass, (3) theft of computer service, (4) personal trespass by computer, and (5) special laws against computer viruses and worms, also known as computer tampering.

D. Federal Cybercrime Enforcement Agencies

What are these agencies? What are their missions?

E. Internet-Based Crimes

Note the types of crimes that can be committed by using the internet.

CAPSTONE CASES: LEARNING ISSUES

United States v. *Corona-Sanchez*

1. Why was the classification of the past conviction for petty theft important to the sentencing process?

2. In the case, the federal judge used the sentencing guidelines, issued under the provisions of the U.S. Sentencing Reform Act of 1984, to determine the appropriate sentence in the case. However, the U.S. Supreme Court held in United States v. Booker (decided 01/12/2005, case no. 04-104) that the Federal Sentencing Guidelines violated the Sixth Amendment. The Court noted that the binding rules set forth in the Guidelines limited the range of sentences that the judge could lawfully impose on a defendant based on the facts found by the jury at his trial. Under present law, the trial judge may use the guidelines as a guide, but he or she is not required to follow them.

Dowling v. *United States*

1. Why is there a problem with determining whether "bootleg" music is stolen property?

2. Why did the court state that federal crimes "are solely creatures of statute?"

Folsum v. *State*

    1.   What are the elements of the crime of burglary?

    2.   Which element is in issue in this case?

    3.   Explain defendant's rationale for making the contention that the marriage relationship and the right of consortium precluded the State, in his case, from ever establishing the nonconsensual entry requisite to the crime of burglary.

People v. *Versaggi*

    1.   Does the conduct of activating existing instructions constitute altering computer programs?

    2.   How did the court define computer tampering under the statute?

PRACTICE TEST QUESTIONS

MULTIPLE CHOICE

____ 10.1.   In order to constitute larceny, the item stolen must have ____ value.
        a. reasonable
        b. commercial
        c. some
        d. intangible

____ 10.2.   The primary difference between larceny and embezzlement is that larceny requires a(n) ____ taking.
        a. lawful
        b. trespassory
        c. consensual
        d. unintentional

____ 10.3   At early common law, under which of the situations listed below could a person be convicted of larceny?
        a. The killing of wild game on the property of another
        b. The cutting and carrying away timber from the property of another
        c. The stealing of harvested timber
        d. The stealing of intangible property

____ 10.4. Property that has a physical form and is capable of being carried away is considered ____ property.
   a. intangible
   b. real
   c. personal and intangible
   d. tangible

____ 10.5. The taking of personal property that has been entrusted to the defendant is considered to be
   a. embezzlement.
   b. larceny.
   c. theft by trick or device.
   d. extortion.

____ 10.6. In the Carrier's Case, the court held that the carrier had rightful possession of the packaged goods under the ____ concept.
   a. misappropriation
   b. non-trespassory taking
   c. actual possession
   d. constructive possession

____ 10.7. The technical term "asportation" refers to the ____ requirement for larceny.
   a. carrying away
   b. possession
   c. specific intent
   d. ownership

____ 10.8. In larceny cases, the phrase "property of another" refers to
   a. ownership of the property.
   b. right of possession by another.
   c. real property only.
   d. None of the above answers are correct.

____ 10.9. The ____ element of the crime of larceny means that the offender intends to permanently deprive the rightful owner of the property in question.
   a. intent to steal
   b. intent to take
   c. claim of right
   d. claim of possession

____ 10.10. A form of theft which involves the transfer of title is
   a. larceny.
   b. embezzlement.

c. false pretenses.

d. burglary.

___ 10.11. The offering, passing, or attempted passing of a forged document with the knowledge that it is false constitutes the crime of

a. larceny.

b. embezzlement.

c. extortion.

d. uttering.

___ 10.12. The gist of the crime of forgery is the

a. act of defrauding.

b. intent to defraud.

c. passing of property.

d. passing of the possession of property.

___ 10.13. Receiving stolen property is a form of

a. larceny.

b. embezzlement.

c. theft.

d. theft by false pretenses.

___ 10.14. Robbery is the unlawful taking of property from the ___ possession of another by force or threat of force.

a. constructive

b. personal

c. implied

d. All of the above answers are correct.

___ 10.15. The unlawful taking of property from a dead person constitutes the crime of

a. embezzlement.

b. extortion.

c. larceny.

d. robbery.

___ 10.16. Backmail is a form of ___ in which a threat is made to disclose a crime or other social disgrace.

a. larceny

b. robbery

c. extortion

d. theft by trick or device.

___ 10.17. The crime of burglary is a wrongful acquisition crime directed against

a. the individual.

b. the owner of the property.

c. the right of possession.

d. property.

___ 10.18. At common law, arson was a crime committed against

a. the individual.

b. the owner of the property.

c. the property.

d. habitation.

___ 10.19. The first federal computer crime law was the

a. Computer Protection Act of 1974.

b. Consumer Protection Act of 1974.

c. Computer Fraud and Abuse Act of 1984.

d. Computer Abuse Act of 1992.

___ 10.20. A set of computer programs, procedures, and associated documentation concerned with the operation of a computer system is known as a

a. data base.

b. computer program.

c. computer software.

d. computer system.

TRUE/FALSE

___ 10.21. At common law, larceny was a capital offense.

___ 10.22. Early common law did not recognize larceny as a crime.

___ 10.23. Larceny requires a wrongful taking of personal property.

___ 10.24. Larceny involves a breach of trust.

___ 10.25. The technical term for "carrying away" is asportation.

___ 10.26. Larceny can only be committed against the person who has possession of the property.

___ 10.27. Forgery is complete when the perpetrator makes a document with the intent to deceive.

___ 10.28. The FBI classifies robbery as a property crime.

____ 10.29. At common law, arson was a capital offense.

____ 10.30. Most of the early defendants in computer crime were able to avoid criminal liability.

KEY CONCEPTS

Identify the below key concepts from Chapter 10 of the text:

_____ 10.1. A trespassory taking and carrying away of personal property.

_____ 10.2. For purposes of theft crimes, a taking without the consent of the victim.

_____ 10-3. Property that can be carried away.

_____ 10.4. Land and fixtures.

_____ 10.5. General term embracing a variety of misconduct by which a person is unlawfully deprived of his or her property.

_____ 10.6. Property that has no intrinsic value.

_____ 10.7. Items that are permanently fixed to the land.

_____ 10.8. The trespassory taking or carrying away the personal property of another with intent to steal the property.

_____ 10.9. Misappropriation of property that is already in the possession of the offender.

_____ 10.10. Unauthorized assumption of the right of ownership.

_____ 10.11. The unlawful taking of property from the person of another by force or fear.

_____ 10.12. Obtaining property by false pretenses.

_____ 10.13. The making of a false document that does not have any apparent legal significance.

_____ 10.14. Offering a forged document with knowledge that the document is false.

_____ 10.15. The alteration of an existing genuine written instrument.

_____ 10.16. The taking of personal property by threat of future harm.

_____ 10.17. Extortion in which a threat is made to disclose a social disgrace.

_____ 10.18. The unauthorized use of another's identity to obtain property.

_____ 10.19. The breaking and entering of a locked automobile.

_____ 10.20. The malicious burning of the personal property of another.

FACTUAL SCENARIOS

1.   Paul steals an expensive watch from the local jewelry store. He knows that Ken needs a watch. At the time Paul stole the watch, he intended to sell it to Ken. As he is leaving the jewelry store, he is apprehended by the police. Paul begs for mercy. He states that he has an agreement to sell any watch that he may steal to Ken. The police tell Paul that if he cooperates, his sentence will be lighter. They give the watch back to Paul. Paul meets Ken and shows Ken the watch. Paul tells Ken that the watch is stolen. Ken buys the watch. Could Ken be convicted of receiving stolen property? Is Paul guilty of larceny?

2.   Susan has a habit of leaving her home unlocked at night. Larry, in order to teach Susan a lesson, enters the home one night by opening the unlocked door. After he is in her home, he notices that she has left her purse on the coffee table. Needing money to pay his rent, he opens the purse and removes $700.00 from the purse. He then leaves the home. What crimes, if any, has he committed?

CROSSWORD 10

Across

4. Attempting to pass a forged document

7. Theft by false ____

11. Larceny from the person or presence of another

12. A form of theft that involves a violation of trust

15. There are five types of ___ crime.

17. The modern trend is to combine all larceny offenses into the crime of ____.

18. Land and fixtures attached to land

19. ___ stolen property

20. Property that is not real

Down

1. The making of a false document

2. Location of trial

3. The wrongful taking of the personal property of another with the intent to steal

5. Movement

6. Unauthorized assumption of the right of ownership

8. Computer crime

9. A taking without consent

10. A form of extortion

13. A willful burning of another's property without authority

14. The taking of personal property by threat of future harm

16. Constructive ____

Chapter 11

Offenses Against the Public Order
and the Administration of Justice

CHAPTER SUMMARY

I. Introduction

This section discusses the First Amendment and the "fighting words" exception.

II. Crimes Against Public Order

Public order offenses are those offenses that disturb or invade society's peace and tranquillity. Public order offenses include breach of peace or disturbing the peace, disorderly conduct, fighting, affray, vagrancy, loitering, carrying weapons, keeping a disorderly house, public intoxication, inciting a riot, rioting, unlawful assembly, rout, obstructing public passage, etc. These offenses are based on the assumption that public order is inherently valuable and should be maintained, and that disorder is not to be tolerated and should be reduced, when it occurs, through application of criminal law.

A. Breach of Peace and Disorderly Conduct

Under common law, the term breach of peace was used to describe any unlawful activity that unreasonably disturbed the peace and tranquilly of the community. Today, breach of peace is a flexible term, occasionally defined by statute, for a violation of a public order, or an act calculated to disturb the public peace. Breach of peace embraces a great variety of conduct destroying or menacing public order and tranquillity. Certain types of conduct may be considered as a breach of peace in one jurisdiction and as disorderly conduct in another.

Whereas breach of peace is a general term, disorderly conduct refers to specific, purposeful, and unlawful behavior that tends to cause public inconvenience, annoyance, or alarm.

B. Fighting and Affray

One form of disorderly conduct is unlawful public fighting. Affray is the fighting of persons in a public place to the terror of the people. Fighting is a mutual event, and differs from assault. If one person attacks another, the attacker may be guilty of assault, since the accosted person may be an innocent victim. But when two people willingly and publicly fight one another, both are guilty of the crime of affray.

C. Public Intoxication

Alcohol abuse is commonplace in American society. The problem is not new to modern times. The idea that alcoholism is a disease was officially endorsed by the American Medical Society in 1956. About 7% of the population have problems with drinking. The economic cost of alcoholism and alcohol-related problems is estimated to be around $100 billion, with most of the cost coming in the form of reduced or lost productivity, and medical and other costs associated with premature death.

D. Alcohol and Drug Laws

Previously, the two most common crimes involving alcohol were public drunkenness and driving while intoxicated. Both crimes are still common. DWI has been expanded to encompass under the influence of drugs and is known as DUI (driving under the influence).

In most jurisdictions there are two separate crimes within the driving under the influence category. First is the driving while under the influence of alcohol or drugs. The second is the driving with a blood alcohol level at or above that specified by statute. The normal blood alcohol level is either 0.10% or 0.08% of blood alcohol content by volume. In many jurisdictions it is illegal to drive while addicted to the use of any drug, unless on an approved drug maintenance program. The term "under the influence" means that alcohol or drugs have so affected the nervous system, the brain, or muscles as to impair to an appreciable degree the ability of the person to operate a motor vehicle in an ordinary and cautious manner. Motor vehicles include cars, vans, trucks, animal-drawn vehicles, go-carts, forklifts, etc.

Public drunkenness is the second most common alcohol-related offense. To constitute the crime, one must, while in a public place, be in a state of intoxication to such a degree that he or she is unable to care for him- or herself. In most cases, it is not a crime to be drunk in a private place. In some jurisdictions, the crime is drunk and disorderly. This crime requires that the person be both drunk and disorderly.

E. Riot and Unlawful Assembly

An unlawful assembly is when three or more persons assemble together for the purpose of doing an unlawful act or a lawful act in a violent, boisterous, or tumultuous manner. It is a specific intent crime and therefore requires that those persons assembled must intend to commit an unlawful act or a lawful act in a prohibited manner.

Rout is a preparatory stage of a riot. A rout is when an unlawful assembly makes an attempt to advance toward the commission of an act which would be a riot. The difference between an unlawful assembly and a rout is that a rout requires an overt act. A riot is the culmination of unlawful assembly and rout, and can be defined as a tumultuous disturbance of the peace by three or more persons assembled of their own authority. A single individual acting alone can commit the crime of urging or inciting a riot. Inciting a riot is the use of words or other means intended and calculated to provoke a riot. The crime of lynching is the taking by means of a riot any person from the lawful custody of any peace officer.

F. Vagrancy and Loitering

At common law, vagrancy was the act of going from place to place by a person without visible means of support, who was idle, and who, though able to work for his or her maintenance, refused to do so, but lived without labor or on the charity of others. The courts have invalidated most of the vagrancy statutes because they punish a status rather than an activity or because they are void for vagueness. Loitering means to delay, to linger, or to idle about a school or public place without lawful business for being present. By specifying the circumstances under which loitering could occur, legislatures have sought to de-emphasize a person's status as a determinant of criminality.

G. Teenage Curfew

The constitutionally of teenage curfew statutes is unclear. The statutes that were overturned by the courts were generally seen as being too vague and as restricting the First Amendment rights of the teenagers.

H. Weapons Carrying

At common law the going about in public armed with a dangerous weapon was a misdemeanor. It was generally accepted, however, that men of quality could lawfully carry and display weapons. Gun control is a controversial topic in the United States. All states have a variety of laws intended to control gun ownership and possession. One common crime is that of carrying a concealed weapon without authorization.

The Brady Law is the most significant federal gun control legislation. The Supreme Court held that the provision which required local law enforcement officers to conduct background checks was unconstitutional. Despite this holding, the main thrust of the Brady Law remains intact. Congress made it a crime for any individual to knowingly possess a firearm in a school zone. This law as also held unconstitutional by the Supreme Court which stated that education in the context of the law was a local and not a national concern.

I. Illegal Entry into the United States

One of the consequences of the terrorist attacks of September 11, 2001 has been a closer examination of individuals entering the United States. Our entry laws are very complex. There are three classes of aliens who are physically present in the United States; those who are legally here, those who are here illegally, and those who are technically regarded as not here at all.

III. Crimes Against the Administration of Government

The third class of social order offenses is that of crimes against the administration of government. Offenses in this category include treason, misprison of treason, rebellion, espionage, sedition, perjury, subornation of perjury, false swearing, bribery, contempt, and misconduct in office.

A. Treason

Treason is an attempt to overthrow the government of the society of which one is a member. At common law an attempt to kill the king or to promote a revolt was considered as high treason. According to the U.S. Constitution, treason against the United States shall consist only in levying war against them, or in adhering to their enemies, giving them aid and comfort. Treason requires some overt act such as affirmative encouragement of the enemy. Disloyal thoughts are not sufficient to constitute treason.

Misprison of treason is the concealment or nondisclosure of the known treason of another. Rebellion consists of deliberate, organized resistance, by force and arms, to the laws or operations of the government, committed by a subject.

Espionage is the gathering, transmitting, or losing information or secrets related to the national defense with the intent or the reasonable belief that such information will be used against the United States. The crime of sedition consists of a communication or agreement intended to defame the government or to incite treason.

B. Perjury and Contempt

Perjury, at common law, was the willful giving of false testimony under oath in a judicial proceedings. Most jurisdictions have enlarged the crime to include any false testimony given under any lawfully administered oath. Some of the jurisdictions call the expanded crime "false swearing."

To constitute perjury or false swearing, the false statement must be material. If the false statement has no bearing on the proceedings, it is not perjury or false swearing. Subordination of perjury occurs when a person procures another to commit perjury.

Criminal contempt consists of deliberate conduct calculated to obstruct or embarrass a court of law, or conduct intended to degrade the role of a judicial officer in administering justice.

C. Obstruction of Justice

Obstruction of justice is an attempt to interfere with the administration of the courts, the judicial system, or law enforcement officers, or with the activities of those who seek justice in a court or whose duties involve the administration of justice.

D. Escape

Escape is the unlawful leaving of official custody or confinement without permission, or the failure to return to custody or confinement following an official temporary leave.

E. Misconduct in Office and Bribery

Misconduct in office occurs when a public official who, under color of law or in his or her official capacity, acts in such a way as to exceed the bounds of his or her office. Doing that which the officer has no right to do is considered as malfeasance. Misfeasance refers to official acts performed improperly, and nonfeasance describes failing to do that which should be done.

Bribery consists of the offense of giving or receiving a gift or reward intended to influence a person in the exercise of a judicial or public duty. Bribery concerns only official acts, and no crime occurs when merely personal actions outside of the official sphere are influenced by a bribe. Generally it is no defense to a bribery charge that the person whom the actor sought to influence was not qualified to act in the desired way.

CAPSTONE CASES: LEARNING ISSUES

Chaplinshy v. *New Hampshire*

1. What is meant by the statement in the opinion that: "Upon appeal, there was a trial *de novo* before a jury?"

2. Why did the defendant contend that the statute was unconstitutional?

3. What does the court mean when it states that the right of free speech is not absolute?

City of Chicago v. *Morales et al.*

1.   Why was the ordinance considered as impermissibly vague?

2.   What does the court mean by the statement that the statute was "invalid on its face?"

Powell v. *Texas*

1.   It is important to distinguish between the ruling in this case and the ruling in Robinson v. California discussed in Chapter 12.

2.   What did the statute in question attempt to prevent? In this case it was the act of being intoxicated in public.

3.   May the State make that act a crime?

PRACTICE TEST QUESTIONS

MULTIPLE CHOICE

___ 11.1.   While breach of peace is a general term, ___ refers to specific, purposeful, and unlawful behavior.
   a. bawdy offenses
   b. breach of peace
   c. disorderly conduct
   d. vagrancy

___ 11.2.   The normal blood alcohol level for most DUBAL crimes is generally
   a. 01.0% or 0.8%.
   b. 0.10% or 0.8 %.
   c. 0.10% or 0.08%.
   d. 0.10% or 0.80%.

___ 11.3.   Which of the crimes listed below is NOT considered a public order offense?
   a. breach of peace
   b. disorderly conduct
   c. drunk in public
   d. treason

___ 11.4.   Contemporary breach of peace statutes are built on the common law emphasis on
   a. fighting words.

b. public tranquillity.
c. offensive words.
d. actual disturbances.

___ 11.5. While disorderly conduct refers to specific, purposeful, and unlawful behavior, _____ is a general term.
a. fighting words
b. offensive words
c. public tranquillity
d. breach of peace

___ 11.6. The term that derives from the word "afraid" and means an altercation that tends to alarm the community is a(n)
a. affray.
b. fight.
c. assault.
d. battery.

___ 11.7. Almost three times as many _____ as _____ are problem drinkers.
a. women, men
b. men, women
c. children, women
d. minors, adults

___ 11.8. The term _____ means driving under the influence of drugs or alcohol or a combination thereof.
a. DWI
b. DUI
c. DUBA
d. DWUBA

___ 11.9. The second must common alcohol-related offense is
a. DUI.
b. DWI.
c. drunk and disorderly.
d. public drunkenness.

___ 11.10 The crime committed when an unlawful assembly makes an attempt to advance toward a riot is a(n)
a. unlawful assembly.
b. disorderly conduct.
c. rout.
d. lynching.

___ 11.11.   At common law, to be a riot at least ____ people must be involved.
a. two
b. three
c. four
d. five

___ 11.12.   The taking of a person from a lawful custody is the gist of the crime of
a. unlawful assembly.
b. disorderly conduct.
c. rout.
d. lynching.

___ 11.13.   The crime of ____ is very similar to the crime of lynching, except that a single individual may commit this offense.
a. rout
b. riot
c. rescuing a prisoner
d. disorderly conduct

___ 11.14.   The common law crime of ____ made it an offense simply to wander from place to place without any visible means of support.
a. disorderly conduct
b. panhandling
c. loitering
d. vagrancy

___ 11.15.   At common law, ____ was really a status rather than an activity.
a. unlawful assembly
b. disorderly conduct
c. vagrancy
d. rout

___ 11.16.   The _____ Act, signed by President Clinton in 1994, provides for a five-day waiting period before the purchase of a handgun.
a. Brady
b. Regan
c. Carter
d. National Gun Control

___ 11.17.   An attempt to overthrow the government of the society of which one is a member is the crime of
a. disloyalty.

b. lynching.

c. routing.

d. treason.

___ 11.18. The crime of _____ consists of advocating the use of unlawful acts as a means of accomplishing a change in industrial ownership or to control political change.

a. criminal syndicalism

b. disloyalty

c. routing

d. perjury

___ 11.19. The willful giving of false testimony under oath in a judicial proceeding constitutes the crime of

a. criminal syndicalism.

b. disloyalty.

c. routing.

d. perjury.

___ 11.20. The failure of a public official to correctly perform official acts considered as

a. malfeasance.

b. misfeasance.

c. nonfeasance.

d. contempt.

TRUE/FALSE

___ 11.21. Fighting words are protected by the First Amendment.

___ 11.22. Prize fighting is the unlawful public fighting undertaken for the purpose of winning an award or prize.

___ 11.23. Intoxication in a private home is generally a crime.

___ 11.24. The normal blood alcohol level for most DUBAL crimes is 01.0% of blood alcohol content by volume.

___ 11.25. Drunk and disorderly crimes generally require that the individual be either drunk or disorderly in a public place.

___ 11.26 The crime of rescuing a prisoner may be committed by a single individual.

___ 11.27. Lynching requires the hanging of the prisoner taken from the custody of law enforcement.

___ 11.28.   At common law, treason was a felony.

___ 11.29.   Espionage is a federal crime.

___ 11.30.   Criminal contempt is the deliberate conduct that was calculated to obstruct or embarrass a court of law.

KEY CONCEPTS

Identify the below key concepts from Chapter 11 of the text:

_____ 11.1.   An unlawful activity that unreasonably disturbs the peace and tranquility of the community.

_____ 11.2.   Specific, purposeful, and unlawful behavior that tends to cause public alarm.

_____ 11.3.   Fighting of persons in a public place to the terror of the people.

_____ 11.4.   Unlawful public fighting for purpose of winning a prize.

_____ 11.5.   An act calculated to disturb the public peace.

_____ 11.6.   Preparatory stage of a riot.

_____ 11.7.   Words which by their very utterance tend to incite an immediate breach of peace.

_____ 11.8.   The taking, by means of riot, any person from the lawful control of law enforcement.

_____ 11.9.   The use of words intended to provoke a riot.

_____ 11.10. A tumultuous disturbance of the peace by three or more persons assembled of their own authority.

_____ 11.11. The act of going from place to place without visible means of support.

_____ 11.12. A person's state of being.

_____ 11.13. The waging of war against one's home country.

_____ 11.14. The unlawful spying for a foreign government.

_____ 11.15. The concealment of a known treason.

_____ 11.16. Giving false testimony in court.

_____ 11.17. An agreement to defame the government.

_____ 11.18. Conduct intended to degrade the role of a judicial officer in administering justice.

_____ 11.19. Opposing a peace officer who is making an arrest.

_____ 11.20. The unlawful leaving of official custody.

FACTUAL SCENARIOS

1.   Carla is testifying as a defense witness in a criminal case involving larceny. The prosecutor asks the following question, "In what year were you born?" Carla's boyfriend is in the courtroom. She did not want him to know her true age. She answered falsely. Two days later she is testifying in a civil case involving the same subject matter. She is asked if she witnessed the defendant attempting to sell the stolen items. She answered falsely. In both cases, she knew that the answers were false. Did her false testimony in the criminal case constitute perjury? Did her false testimony in the civil case constitute the crime of perjury? Does it make any difference that the second case was a civil, not criminal, case?

2.   Sherry, a 14-year-old girl, was stopped by the police and questioned regarding a stolen bicycle. As she was leaving the police presence, she turned around and said to the police officer, "F--- you, you pig." The officer arrested her and charged her with disorderly conduct under a Minnesota statute that not only prohibited "fighting words," but also prohibited words merely intended to cause alarm, anger, or, create resentment in others. The trial court found that the words directed toward the police officer were unlikely to provoke a violent reaction or incite an immediate breach of the peace. The court also found that the words were intended to create resentment by the police officer. She appeals her adjudication in juvenile court as a delinquent child (guilty of a criminal offence). Should her conviction be reversed?

116

CROSSWORD 11

Across

1. The act of making war against your government

4. Alcohol and ___ laws

5. __ of peace

8. The taking of a person from lawful custody

11. Spying

13. A person's state of being

15. __ and disorderly

16. Giving a gift to influence a public officer

18. The act of willfully giving false testimony in court

Down

2. An agreement intended to incite treason

3. ___ words

6. Disorderly conduct in court

7. Driving under the influence of ___

9. A common law crime based on status

10. The preparatory state of a riot

12. Public ___ offenses

14. The fighting of persons in a public place to the terror of the people

17. A tumultuous disturbance of the peace

Chapter 12

Offenses Against Public Morality

CHAPTER SUMMARY

I. Introduction

Consider the problems with regulating certain conduct like nudity.

II. Crimes Against Public Decency and Morality

While most crimes have specific and identifiable individual victims, some crimes do not. Those crimes are called crimes against public decency and morality. The laws regulating these crimes are targeted against behavior which negatively impacts public decency and morality. They originated in medieval times, when secular rulers and church leaders became concerned with institutionalizing accepted notions of good and evil, and especially with controlling human sexual behavior to have it conform to existing notions of propriety.

Crimes against public decency and morality are sometimes referred to as victimless crimes by virtue of the fact that they generally involving willing participants. A victimless crime may be defined as an offense committed against the social values and interests represented in and protected by the criminal law, and in which the parties to the offense willingly participate.

A. Prostitution

Prostitution is said to be the world's oldest profession. In early England, it was an ecclesiastical crime and not a criminal offense. Prostitution is generally defined as the offering or receiving of the body for sexual intercourse for hire. An offer to perform the act, or consent to do so, is generally sufficient to constitute prostitution. Soliciting prostitution is the act of asking, enticing, or requesting another to commit the crime of prostitution. In most situations, voluntary sexual intercourse between consenting adults is not a crime. It is the act of solicitation and payment for sexual services that violates criminal law.

The crime of promoting prostitution is a statutory offense in almost all jurisdictions. It is designed to punish persons who profit or attempt to profit by using others to engage in prostitution. Pandering occurs when a person solicits a person to perform an act of prostitution or when he or she knowingly assembles persons at a fixed place for the purpose of being solicited by others to perform an act of prostitution.

B. Pornography, Obscenity, and Lewdness

All jurisdictions have statutes which punish the sale, possession, and distribution of obscene material, and most have statutes defining lewdness or public indecency. Pornography is the depiction of sexual behavior in such a way as to excite the viewer sexually. Obscenity may be defined as that which appeals to the prurient interest and lacks serious literary, artistic, political or scientific value.

To be obscene and not protected by the free speech clause, objectionable material must meet all the following requirements: (1) the average person, applying contemporary community standards, would find that the work, taken as a whole, appeals to the prurient interest; (2) the work depicts or describes, in a patently offensive way, sexual conduct specifically defined by the applicable statute; and (3) the work, taken as a whole, lacks serious literary, artistic, political, or scientific value. Prurient interest means an obsession with lascivious and immoral matters.

One special area of concern is the sexual exploitation of children or child pornography. The U.S. Supreme Court has held that a New York law against the distribution of child pornography was valid even though the material in question did not appeal to the prurient interest of the average person and was not displayed in what could be regarded as a patently offensive manner.

Whereas pornography refers to some thing that is obscene, lewdness refers to behavior that is obscene. Lewd behavior consists of intimate activity by a single individual where such activity is intended to be sexually arousing. Lewd behavior is sometimes referred to as lasciviousness or indecent exposure.

C. Other Consensual Sex Offenses

Fornication and adultery continue to exist as crimes in many states. The U.S. Supreme Court upheld a Georgia statute that imposed criminal sanctions on acts that occur in the privacy of one's own bedroom. Fornication is voluntary sexual intercourse with another person by unmarried persons.

Homosexuality has traditionally been viewed as unnatural sexual behavior and frequently considered as a crime against nature. Bestiality is sexual relations with animals. Buggery is understood to mean anal intercourse. Sodomy is the carnal knowledge of any person by the anus or mouth of another. Bigamy is the crime of marrying one person while still married to another person. Bigamy is a crime against the family. Polygamy is the marrying of, or cohabiting with, more than one spouse at a time in the purported exercise of the right of plural marriage. Incest is unlawful sexual intercourse with a relative through blood or marriage.

D. Gambling and Gaming

Gambling is the wagering of money, or of some other thing of value, on the outcome or occurrence of an event. It is illegal where made so by law. Gambling was not a crime at common law. Gambling is also called gaming in recognition of the fact that it may involve games of chance. Gambling and gaming are heavily regulated by both state and federal statutes.

E. Controlled Substances

"Drug" is a generic term applicable to a wide variety of substances having any physical or psychotropic effect upon the human body. Drugs have been defined by social convention. The two major classes of drugs are those which are biologically active and those which are psychologically active. Controlled substance refers to specifically defined bioactive or psychoactive chemical substances which come under the purview of the criminal law.

Anti-drug legislation in the U.S. dates back to around 1875. The Harrison Act in 1914 was the first major federal legislation. That act permitted physicians to prescribe controlled substances for the purposes of medical treatment. The basis of federal drug enforcement is the Comprehensive Drug Abuse Prevention and Control Act of 1970 (CSA). The CSA establishes five schedules which classify psychoactive drugs according to their degree of psychoactivity and abuse potential.

Anti-drug laws at the state level show a surprising degree of uniformity. Most have adopted some form of the Uniform Controlled Substances Act. The possession of drugs listed in schedules I and II are generally felonies, while the possession of drugs listed in schedules III to V may be either felonies or misdemeanors. Generally speaking, the elements of unlawful possession of a controlled substance are: (1) possession (except as provided by law), (2) of any controlled substance, and (3) unless upon the written prescription of a physician, dentist, etc.

Asset forfeiture is an enforcement strategy used to seize all monies, negotiable instruments, or other things of value furnished or intended to be furnished by any person in exchanged for a controlled substance and all proceeds traceable to any such exchange. Forfeiture statutes find a legal basis in the relation-back doctrine. The relation-back doctrine assumes that because the government's right to illicit proceeds relate back to the time they are generated, anything acquired through the expenditure of those proceeds also belong to the government.

Many states have passed legislation allowing therapeutic-research programs involving the use of marijuana. California passed Proposition 215 which allows doctors to prescribe marijuana for medicinal purposes. Arizona has passed similar legislation. Many believe that this will force the government to change its stand on marijuana.

F. A Critique of Laws Regulating Public Morality

Legal scholars have criticized the notion of crimes against public decency and morality, calling them legal moralism. American legislative history shows that law-making bodies across the country have generally assumed the authority to criminalize any conduct which they thought might be damaging to the health, safety, and morality of the community. Understand the problems with attempting to legislate public morality.

CAPSTONE CASES: LEARNING ISSUES

City of Erie v. *Pap's A.M.*

1. Should nude dancing be protected under the First Amendment? Justify your opinion.

2. When is a case moot according to the court?

3. What is the "O'Brien's four-factor" test?

Lawrence v. *Texas*

1. What three questions did the Supreme Court consider when it granted the writ to review the case?

2. What were the reasons given by the Court in overruling *Bowers v. Hardwick*?

United States v. *Thomas*

1. Did the court find that the sending of obscene material over the internet constituted the transportation of the material in interstate commerce?

2. What definition of "community" did the court use?

PRACTICE TEST QUESTIONS

MULTIPLE CHOICE

____ 12.1. An individual commits the crime of ____ by soliciting a person to perform an act of prostitution.

a. promoting prostitution
b. pandering
c. pimping
d. The conduct may constitute a violation of all three crimes.

___ 12.2. The word ___ comes from the Latin word *porne* (prostitute).
a. obscenity
b. prostitute
c. prostitution
d. pornography

___ 12.3. The depiction of sexual behavior in such a way as to excite the viewer sexually is defined as
a. obscenity.
b. prostitute.
c. prostitution.
d. pornography.

___ 12.4. Generally, voluntary sexual intercourse between adults is ___ crime.
a. a felony
b. a misdemeanor
c. a minor
d. not a

___ 12.5. The leading case which defines obscenity is
a. *Stanley* v. *Georgia*.
b. *Miller* v. *California*.
c. *Bowers* v. *Harwick*.
d. *Board of Education* v. *Barnette*.

___ 12.6. In the case of ____, the U.S. Supreme Court upheld a Georgia statute that imposed criminal sanctions on homosexual acts that occur in the privacy of one's own bedroom and was overruled by *Lawrence* v. *Texas*.
a. *Stanley* v. *Georgia*
b. *Miller* v. *California*
c. *Bowers* v. *Harwick*

___ 12.7. Crimes against public decency and morality are sometimes referred to as ____ crimes.
a. public offense
b. policy
c. decency
d. victimless

___ 12.8   In 1997, the Supreme Court found key provisions of the Communications Decency
            Act unconstitutional because they
            a. did not involve interstate commerce.
            b. were too vague.
            c. did not appeal to the prurient interest of the average person.
            d. unduly prohibited free speech.

___ 12.9   Lewd and lascivious conduct is sometimes termed "public indecency" or
            a. prostitution.
            b. obscenity.
            c. lewdness.
            d. indecent exposure.

___ 12.10   _____ occurs when two unmarried persons have sexual relations.
            a. Adultery
            b. Bestiality
            c. Buggery
            d. Fornication

___ 12.11. ___ has generally been understood to mean anal intercourse.
            a. Adultery
            b. Bestiality
            c. Buggery
            d. Fornication

___ 12.12   Unlawful sexual intercourse with a blood relative is considered as
            a. adultery.
            b. bigamy.
            c. polygamy.
            d. incest.

___ 12.13. The offense of marrying more than one spouse at a time is the crime of
            a. adultery.
            b. bigamy.
            c. polygamy.
            d. incest.

___ 12.14   Gambling which involves games of chance or by luck is frequently referred to as
            a. betting.
            b. gaming.
            c. numbers.
            d. touting.

___ 12.15   A generic term that is applicable to a wide variety of substances that have physical or psychotropic effects upon the human body is
a. controlled substance.
b. drug.
c. percursors.
d. Rohypnol.

___ 12.16.   The term that refers to specifically defined bioactive or psychoactive chemical substances which come under the purview of the criminal law is
a. controlled substance.
b. drug.
c. percursors.
d. Rohypnol.

___ 12.17.   Funitrazepam, also known as ___, is more commonly known as the date rape drug.
a. controlled substance
b. drug
c. percursors
d. Rohypnol

___ 12.18.   Chemicals that may be used in the manufacture of a controlled substance are known as
a. controlled substance.
b. drug.
c. percursors.
d. Rohypnol.

___ 12.19.   The use of ____ in classifying controlled substance is an attempt to categorize controlled substances according to their potential for abuse.
a. abuse classifications
b. definitions
c. classses
d. schedules

___ 12.20.   The craving for a specific drug which results from long-term substance abuse is considered to be
a. physical addiction.
b. psychological addiction.
c. non-substance addiction.
d. controlled addiction.

____ 12.21.   At early English law, prostitution was not a common law crime.

____ 12.22.   In all jurisdictions, a conviction for prostitution requires that the sexual act in question must actually take place.

____ 12.23.   The crime of promoting prostitution is a statutory offense in almost all jurisdictions.

____ 12.24.   The U.S. Supreme Court held in *Stanley* v. *Georgia* that obscenity is protected under the First Amendment free speech guarantee.

____ 12.25.   The "right of privacy" protects the public exhibition of obscene matter.

____ 12.26.   Lascivious means that which is obscene or lewd, or which tends to cause lust.

____ 12.27.   Gambling was a common law crime.

____ 12.28.   Hard drugs include those drugs which have any potential for abuse and addiction.

____ 12.29.   The Harrison Act was the first major federal act involving the use of drugs.

____ 12.30.   Marijuana is a Schedule I drug.

KEY CONCEPTS

Identify the below key concepts from Chapter 12 of the text:

_____ 12.1.   Sexual intercourse for hire.

_____ 12.2.   A morbid interest in sex.

_____ 12.3.   Depiction of sexual behavior in such a way as to excite the viewer sexually.

_____ 12.4.   Material which appeals to the prurient interest and lacks serious literary, artistic, political, or scientific value.

_____ 12.5.   Soliciting a person to perform an act of prostitution.

_____ 12.6.   Obscene behavior.

_____ 12.7. Sexual intercourse that occurs between two persons, one of whom is unmarried.

_____ 12.8. The act of procuring a prostitute for another.

_____ 12.9. Sexual intercourse that occurs between two persons, one of whom is married to another individual.

_____ 12.10. Carnal knowledge of any person by the anus.

_____ 12.11. Depiction of sexual behavior involving children.

_____ 12.12. Marrying one person while still legally married to someone else.

_____ 12.13. An obsession with lascivious and immoral matters.

_____ 12.14. Having more than one spouse at the same time.

_____ 12.15. Unlawful sexual intercourse with a brother or sister.

_____ 12.16. Chemicals that may be used in the manufacturer of a controlled substance.

FACTUAL SCENARIOS

1.   Linda is hungry and without a place to sleep. She approaches John and tells him that she will have sex with him for $50.00. John, an undercover police officer, arrests her for prostitution. She is released after spending the night in jail. The next day, still hungry and without a place to sleep, she approaches Jim. She tells Jim that she will sleep with him if he will buy her dinner and pay for the hotel room. Jim, another undercover agent, arrests her for prostitution. Has she committed prostitution by her statements to Jim?

2.   Jimmy loves to gamble. He places bets on all the baseball games. The bets are placed with a local bookie, in violation of state law. A friend, in an attempt to cure Jimmy of his addiction to gambling, bets Jimmy that he cannot go two weeks without placing a bet on a baseball game. Is this bet an illegal bet? Jimmy wins the bet. During the two weeks he discovers that buying and selling futures in the grain market involves more risk than betting on baseball games. Would he be involved in illegal gambling if he devotes his gambling to buying and selling futures in the gain market?

CROSSWORD 12

Across

3. Obscene

8. __ substances

9. Aiding others in the committing prostitution

11. Law designed to fight organized crime

17. Carnal knowledge of another by the anus or with the mouth

19. The crime of marrying one person while still married to another

20. Sexual intercourse with a close relative

21. Sex for hire

Down

1. Sexual intercourse between male and female one of whom is married to another person

2. A crime in which all parties to the offense willingly participate.

4. The depiction of sexual behavior in such a way as to excite the viewer's sexuality

5. Anal intercourse

6. Gambling

7. Soliciting a person to perform an act of prostitution

10. Sexual intercourse between unmarried persons

12. Sex with animals

13. The act of asking another to commit the crime of prostitution

14. Crimes against ___

15. ___ exposure

16. That which appeals to the prurient interests and lacks serious literary, artistic, political, or scientific value

18. Morbid interest

127

Chapter 13

Victims and the Law

Chapter Summary

I. Introduction

Consider the Carpenter case and how anyone may be the victim of a crime.

II. Who Is a Victim?

The word victim denotes someone who has been harmed through the kind of activity proscribed by the criminal law. Victim means any individual against whom an offense has been committed under the Violent Crime Control and Law Enforcement Act of 1994. It also includes a parent or legal guardian if the victim is below the age of 18 or incompetent and one or more family members or relatives designated by the court if the victim is deceased or incapacitated. The Federal Bureau of Prisons defines "victim" as someone who suffers direct or threatened physical, emotional, or financial harm as the result of the commission of a crime.

III. A Short History of the Victim

For much of early human history victims had few, if any, official support mechanisms. Early social norms, however, supported the actions of victims. Early tribal codes generally required offenders' families to care for the needs of victims or their survivors. This early period was referred to as the Golden Age of the Victim. Eventually crimes came to be seen as offenses against society, and the needs of the victim were forgotten. Until the 1960s, victims were expected only to provide evidence of a crime and to testify against those who had offended them.

Renewed interest in victims in the 1960s led to a resurgence of efforts meant to assist them. The first modern victim compensation act was adopted by New Zealand. California enacted the first American statute. Modern victim compensation programs require applicants to meet certain eligibility requirements, and most set award maximums.

A. The Philosophy of Victim Compensation

There are seven different schools of thought regarding victim compensation programs. They are: (1) strict liability, (2) government negligence theory, (3) equal protection theory,

(4) humanitarian theory, (5) social welfare theory, (6) crime prevention theory, and (7) political motives.

B. Victims' Assistance Programs Today

Victims' assistance programs are designed to provide comfort and assistance to victims of crime. Most programs are small and staffed by local volunteers. They provide a variety of services to victims including explaining court process, providing court escorts, helping victims compete compensation forms, educating the public, advocating with employers on behalf of victims, and providing transportation to victims.

Two large nonprofit public groups that serve the needs of victims on a national scale are NOVA and NCVC. NOVA was founded in 1975 and it is a private, non-profit, umbrella organization working on behalf of victims of crime and disaster. NCVC was begun in 1985 with the mission to serve as a national resource center for victims and their advocates, to establish training programs, and to encourage and promote research concerning victims of violent crime.

IV. Victims' Rights Legislation

The federal Victim and Witness Protection Act of 1982 was enacted to enhance and protect the necessary role of crime victims and witnesses in the criminal justice process. The most significant federal legislation to date is the 1984 Victims of Crime Act, which resulted from recommendations made by the President's Task Force on Victims of Crime. In addition, the Violent Crime Control and Law Enforcement Act of 1994 contained significant victims' rights legislation.

A. The Growth of Victims' Rights

Victims' advocates established a platform of victims rights involving six basic principles. More than 30 states have enacted legislation or modified their constitutions in recognition of victims' rights.

B. "Son of Sam" Laws

The "Son of Sam" laws, also known as notoriety-for-profit statutes, are intended to deny convicted offenders the opportunity to further capitalize on their crimes by setting the stage for civil action against the infamous offenders who might otherwise profit from the sale of their "story." Most states hold potential profits in an escrow account, allowing victims or their survivors the time necessary to file a suit.

C. Victim Impact Statements

Victim impact statements are a result of the victim rights movement. Victim impact statements generally take the form of written documents which describe the losses, suffering, and trauma experienced by crime victims or by their surviving family members. Judges are expected to consider them in arriving at an appropriate sanction for the offender.

The constitutionality of victim impact statements have been challenged in several cases. In 1987, the U.S. Supreme Court held that information in victim impact statements leads to the risk that the death penalty might be imposed in an arbitrary and capricious manner. In 1991, however, the Court held that victim impact evidence is simply another form or method of informing the sentencing authority about the specific harm caused by the crime in question.

V. Victim Statistics

Two major surveys provide annual crime statistics for the United States. They are the UCR and the NCVS. The UCR is based on reports by law enforcement agencies to the FBI, and the NCVS is based upon victim self-reports. Comparisons between the two are difficult.

A. The National Crime Victimization Survey

The NCVS is the government's primary source of information about criminal victimization. About twice a year, data are obtained from a nationally representative sample. The Bureau of Justice Statistics annually polls people over the age of 12 about rape, robbery, assault, larceny, burglary, assault, and motor vehicle theft. The findings report the likelihood of victimization by rape, sexual assault, robbery, etc., for the population as a whole, as well as special segments of the population such as women.

B. Violence Against Women

The NCVS were redesigned in 1992 to produce more accurate reporting of incidents of rape and sexual assault and of crimes committed by intimates or family members. According to the results, women annually sustain about five million violent victimizations. Many of them were committed by intimates or other family members. Annually, there are about 500,000 rapes and sexual assaults reported to interviewers. Most are committed by friends or acquaintances. Women ages 19 to 29 and women in families with low incomes are more likely than other women to be victims of violence by an intimate.

C. Young Black Male Victims

Black males ages 12 to 24 experience violent crime at a rate significantly higher than the rates for other population groups. Black males ages 16 to 19 are particularly at risk, and have violent victimization rates double that of white males and three times that of white females in the same age group. While the rate of violent victimizations experienced by young white males has remained relatively constant over the past decade, it has increased substantially for young black males.

D. Elderly Victims

Persons aged 65 and older have the lowest victimization rates for all types of crime. While they comprise about 14% of all persons interviewed in the surveys, they report less that 2% of all victimizations. Not only are the rates low among the elderly, they have been declining.

E. The Uniform Crime Reports

The Uniform Crime Reports have been in existence since the early 1930s. The reports are based on crimes reported by law enforcement agencies to the FBI. Crimes are divided into two major categories, Part I Offenses and Part II Offenses. Part I Offenses consist of eight major crimes: murder, rape, robbery, aggravated assault, burglary, auto theft, and arson. Part I is also divided into violent crimes and property crimes. The UCR Crime Index is a rate-based measure which sums the total of all Part I offenses divided by the total population. Part II offenses, which consist of 19 lesser crimes, are counted only in terms of arrests. The highest arrest counts were for larceny-theft and drug abuse violations.

VI. Restitution

The President's Task Force on Victims of Crime recognized the inequitable financial consequences that often follow criminal victimization. The task force report recommended that mandates be established requiring judges to order that convicted offenders be required to pay restitution in cases where the victims have suffered financially, unless compelling reasons to the contrary could be demonstrated. An original proponent of restitution as a sentencing philosophy was Stephen Schafer. He listed three types of restitution; compensatory fines, double or treble damages, and restitution in lieu of other punishment.

A. The Restoration Movement

The maturing of the victims movement led to the development of the concept of restoration. Restorative justice builds upon restitution and other sentencing strategies to benefit all parties impacted by the criminal event: the victim, society, and the offender. A restorative program requires the offender to make reparations to the victim and the community. Restorative justice holds that it is necessary to attain a balance between the legitimate needs of the community, the offender, and the victim.

CAPSTONE CASES: LEARNING ISSUES

Simon & Schuster v. *State Crime Victims Board*

1. What is the purpose of the "Son of Sam" laws?

2. Why did the court find that the statute was presumptively inconsistent with the First Amendment if it imposes a financial burden on speakers because of the context of the speech?

PRACTICE TEST QUESTIONS

MULTIPLE CHOICE

___ 13.1. When was the "Golden Age of the Victim"?
a. the 1950s
b. the 1960s
c. the 1970s
d. prior to 1700

___ 13.2. The first American victim compensation statute was adopted by ____ in 1965.
a. California
b. New York
c. New Jersey
d. Texas

___ 13.3. Which of the two below listed groups are nonprofit public groups that serve the needs of victims on a national scale?
a. CVA and NVA
b. COBA and VOCA
c. NOVA and NCVC
d. NOVA and VOCA

___ 13.4. The recommendations of the President's Task Force on Victims of Crime resulted in the passage of the

a. CVA.
b. NOVA.
c. VOCA.
d. Violence Against Women Act.

____ 13.5. What are the two major surveys used in the United States to provide annual crime statistics?
a. FBI and UCR
b. NOVA and SOV
c. NCVS and NOVA
d. NCVS and UCR

____ 13.6. Which household group suffers higher rates of property victimization for all types of property crime?
a. Asians
b. Blacks
c. Native Americans
d. Hispanics

____ 13.7. The elderly appear to be particularly susceptible to what type of crime?
a. crimes involving personal violence
b. crimes involving economic gain
c. crimes involving homicides
d. crimes involving automobiles

____ 13.8. Which group of robbery victims is more likely to report the crime to police?
a. young Black males
b. young white males
c. men and women over the age of 65
d. women under the age of 65

____ 13.9. Which of the below statements is correct regarding the Uniform Crime Reports?
a. Part II offenses are considered as the major crimes.
b. Part I offenses include prostitution.
c. Part II offenses include rape.
d. The Crime Index is a rate-based measure which sums the total of all Part I offenses divided by the total population.

____ 13.10. Which of the below statements is correct regarding the UCR Crime Index?
a. It is not a rate-based measure.
b. It is a measurement of Part II offenses per 100,000.

c. It is the total of all Part I offenses divided by the population and expressed as per 100,000.

d. None of the above statements are correct.

____ 13.11. Which of the below listed crimes is a Part I offense under the Uniform Crime Reports?
a. car theft
b. forgery
c. child abuse
d. fraud

____ 13.12. If a city has a robbery rate of 26.1 for the UCR Crime Index, what does this means?
a. There were over 26 robberies committed in that city that year.
b. For the past five years there have been an average of 26.1 robberies per year.
c. There were 26.1 robberies for every 1,000,000 residents.
d. There were 261 robberies for every 10,000 residents.

____ 13.13. The restoration movement builds upon restitution and other sentencing strategies to benefit ____ who were impacted by the criminal event.
a. offenders
b. victims
c. relatives
d. all parties

____ 13.14. The first state to enact a Son of Sam law was
a. California.
b. New York.
c. Texas.
d. Washington.

____ 13.15. The original Son of Sam was?
a. David Berkowitz.
b. Sam Berkowitz.
c. David Wilson.
d. Sam Wilson.

TRUE/FALSE

____ 13.16. Throughout much of early human history, victims had many official support mechanisms.

_____ 13.17. The Golden Age of Victims emerged under the period known as the "King's Peace."

_____ 13.18. England adopted the first modern victim compensation statute.

_____ 13.19. Presently, every state has some form of victim compensation legislation.

_____ 13.20. Most victim/witness assistance programs are small and staffed by volunteers.

_____ 13.21. NOVA is a private for-profit, umbrella organization.

_____ 13.22. The right of allocation involves the right to speak at the sentencing hearing.

_____ 13.23. Today's Son of Sam laws attempt to prohibit criminals from capitalizing on their criminal notoriety in the mass media.

_____ 13.24. The NCVS excludes many crimes which are counted by the UCR.

_____ 13.25. The NCVS is the government's primary source of information about criminal victimization.

KEY CONCEPTS

Identify the below key concepts from Chapter 13 of the text:

_____ 13.1. An historical epoch during which victims had well-recognized rights.

_____ 13.2. A survey that provides data on surveyed households that report they were affected by crime.

_____ 13.3. Person designated by a court in cases where the victim is deceased, normally a close family member.

_____ 13.4. Individual against whom a crime has been committed.

_____ 13.5. Secondary victimization.

_____ 13.6. National Center for Victims of Crime.

_____ 13.7. Statutory provision permitting crime victims to speak at the sentencing of convicted offenders.

_____ 13.8. A summation of crime statistics tallied annually by the FBI.

_____ 13.9. Notoriety-for-profit laws.

_____ 13.10. Major crimes considered in the UCRs.

_____ 13.11. A written document prepared for court that describes the suffering and loss caused by a defendant's commission of a crime against the victim.

_____ 13.12. A group of lesser crimes included in the UCRs.

FACTUAL SCENARIOS

1.   Jerry steals $2,000 from his elderly neighbor. The neighbor, because of the theft, is unable to pay his utilities: the telephone and electric power. The neighbor borrows money at a high interest rate and has his telephone and power reconnected. The utilities assess him $200.00 in late payments and reconnecting fees. The neighbor also is required to pay $150.00 in interest on the loan. The jurisdiction is involved in the restorative movement. As court services officer, you must prepare a recommendation to the judge as how to handle the sentencing aspect of this case. Jerry is a retired school teacher and receives $700.00 per month as his sole income. What factors should you consider in formulating your recommendations to the judge?

2.   David's father is killed by the defendant during a bank robbery. David attends the trial. After the defendant is convicted of murder, David requests that he be allowed to present a statement to the judge before the defendant is sentenced. What rights does David have in this regard?

CROSSWORD 13

Across

3. ___ I Offenses

6. The right to speak at sentencing

10. Crimes of ___

11. Data

13. Victims of Crime Act

14. National Victim's Center

15. Victim's ___ programs

16. Widely known

Down

1. Age group least likely to be a victim

2. ___ Age of the Victim

4. Victim's ___

5. Payments to victims

7. National Organization for Victim's Assistance

8. Person injured in a violent crime

9. National Crime Victimization Survey

12. ___ of Sam

17. Office of Victims of Crime

Chapter 14

Punishment and Sentencing

CHAPTER SUMMARY

I. Introduction

Sentencing is the process through which a sentencing authority imposes a lawful punishment or other sanction upon a person convicted of violating the criminal law.

II. Sentencing Rationales

One way of distinguishing crimes from civil violations is to recognize that crimes are subject to punishment. Hart identifies five distinguishing features of criminal punishment. Those five features are: (1) it must involve pain or other consequences normally considered unpleasant, (2) it must be for an offense against legal rules, (3) it must be of an actual or supposed offender for his offense, (4) it must be intentionally administered by human beings other than the offender, and (5) it must be imposed and administered by an authority constituted by a legal system against which the offense is committed. The just deserts is a popular model of criminal sentencing which holds that criminal offenders deserve the punishment that they receive at the hands of the state, and suggests that punishments should be appropriate to the type and severity of crime committed.

A. Retribution

Retribution is the most punishment oriented of all sentencing goals and underlies the just deserts philosophy. It is a straightforward theory of punishment. The state is justified in punishing because and only because offenders deserve it. The purpose of retribution is to get back at the offender by meting out a punishment which is in some primal way satisfying to the social group and to the victim or his or her survivors.

B. Deterrence

Deterrence, like retribution, also depends upon the imposition of punishment, but for a different purpose. Punishment is seen as a powerful inhibitor, capable of keeping behavior in line. There are two types of deterrence: specific and general. Specific deterrence is intended to deter the individual sentenced to punishment from committing future offenses. General deterrence uses punishment as an example to others who may be contemplating breaking the law. Critics of deterrence say that there is little evidence that punishment deters criminal behavior.

C. Rehabilitation

The purpose of rehabilitation is to reform the criminal offenders, restoring them to productive lives within the community. Rehabilitation programs, which may also involve a punishment component, often include jobs or skills training, educational course work, counseling, and psychological treatment.

D. Restoration

Restoration emphasizes the emotional and financial cost of crime to its victims, and seeks to restore crime victims to a state akin to that which they were in prior to victimization. It is a sentencing goal which attempts to make victims and the community whole again. The emphasis today is on the notion of restorative justice. This concept identifies a triad of needs: (1) the need to compensate victims, (2) the need to place appropriate responsibility on the offender, and (3) the need to attempt reintegration of the offender with the community.

E. Incapacitation

Incapacitation is a strategy which makes use of imprisonment or some other sentencing option to reduce the likelihood that an offender will be capable of committing future offenses. Incapacitation is based on the premise that those who are removed from the community, particularly through incarceration, cannot victimize society during a time of physical separation. Incapacitation is embodied in habitual offender statutes.

III. Imposing Criminal Sanctions

In most cases, the sentencing authority is the judge. In some states, like Texas, juries may be called upon to impose an appropriate sentence. Until recently, judges had considerable leeway in sentencing decisions. Until the last 30 years, indeterminate sentencing was followed in most jurisdictions. An indeterminate sentence is a sentence to imprisonment where the period of commitment is for a range of time. A consecutive sentence is where one of two or more sentences imposed at the same time, after conviction for more than one offense, and which is served is sequence with the other sentences. A concurrent sentence is one which is served at the same time another sentence is being served.

Most states and the federal government have switched to determinate sentencing. A determinate sentence sets a single standard time quantity of imprisonment. These are also called fixed sentences. Determinate sentencing incorporates the principles of proportionality, equity, and social debt by standardizing sentences according to offense severity and criminal history. In determining the appropriate determinate sentence to impose, the sentencing authority considers aggravating and mitigating factors. Aggravating factors are circumstances relating to the commission of a crime which cause its gravity to be greater than that of the average instance of the given type of offense. Mitigating factors are circumstances surrounding commission of a crime which do not in law justify or excuse the act, but which in fairness may be considered as reducing the blameworthiness of the defendant.

A. Federal Sentencing Practices

The Sentencing Reform Act of 1984 established the U.S. Sentencing Commission and mandated the development of determinate sentencing guidelines. The guidelines combine the seriousness of an offense with an offender's past criminal record in computing the length of prison time to which a federal court should sentence a convicted offender. The U.S. Supreme Court in *United States* v. *Booker*, decided 01/12/2005, held that sentencing guidelines were not required to be followed by the trial judge. Booker stated that a federal trial judge may refer to the guideline in determining the sentence, but is not required to follow them.

B. Truth in Sentencing

The federal Comprehensive Crime Control Act of 1984 addressed the issue of honesty in sentencing for all federal offenders. The federal emphasis on honesty in sentencing was emulated by many states. The idea that sentences that are imposed should closely match the time inmates actually serve is called truth in sentencing. It has become an important policy focus of many state legislatures and the federal Congress.

C. Determinate Sentencing under Attack

Although determinate sentencing is now the ascendant philosophy in the federal and state jurisdictions, it has recently come under attack by those who claim that determinate sentencing practices unfairly eliminate the discretion of sentencing authorities, and that such practices do not sufficiently distinguish between offenders according to the degree of blameworthiness of their crimes or the moral character of individual offenders. As some claim, federal guidelines have created an assembly line system for dispensing justice that is rigid and mechanical.

IV. Plea Bargaining

Many sentences are imposed as a result of bargained pleas. Plea bargaining circumvents the trial process and dramatically reduces the time required for the resolution of a criminal case. Without plea bargaining most criminal courts would become mired in the legal formalities required by trials, and case backlogs would increase substantially.

V. Traditional Sentencing Options

Sentencing is fundamentally a risk management strategy designed to protect the public while serving the ends of rehabilitation, deterrence, retribution, and restoration. The goals of sentencing are difficult to agree on. The four traditional sanctions which continue to dominate the thinking of most legislators and judges when dealing with criminal law. The four traditional sanctions are: imprisonment, probation, fines, and death. Fines, imprisonment, and probation are generally available to judges in most sentencing situations. Probation is a sentence to imprisonment that is deferred. Death penalty is an option in most jurisdictions, but only for a select group of offenders.

VI. Capital Punishment

Capital punishment is the most extreme sentencing option available in the United States. It was absent from federal law for a number of years until its reestablishment under the 1988 Anti-Drug Abuse Act which included the possibility of capital punishment for drug-related murders. In 1994, the number of federal crimes punishable by the death penalty was increased to approximately 60. Capital punishment can be analyzed from three quite different points of view. They are: (1) legal perspective, (2) philosophical, moral, and ethical perspective, and (3) via empirical analysis of data on deterrence, public opinion, and the like.

A. The Courts and Capital Punishment

In 1972, the U.S. Supreme Court ruled that the "evolving standards of decency" necessitated a reconsideration of the Eighth Amendment guarantees. The Court, in a 5 to 4 decision, invalidated Georgia's death penalty statute on the basis that it allowed a jury unguided discretion in the imposition of the death penalty. In 1976, the Court approved Georgia's newly developed two-step trial procedure. As result, death penalty trials in most jurisdictions involve two stages. In the first stage, guilt or innocence is decided. If the defendant is convicted of a capital crime, a second or penalty phase ensues. The penalty phase permits the introduction of new evidence that may have been irrelevant to the question of guilt, but which may be relevant to punishment, such as drug use or childhood abuse.

B. Limits on Death Row Appeals

In a move to reduce delays in the carrying out of death sentences, the U.S. Supreme Court limited the number of appeals a condemned person may bring to the federal courts. The Court held that repeated filings for the sole purpose of delay promotes disrespect for the finality of convictions. The Court established a two-pronged criterion for future appeals. In any petition beyond the first, filed with a federal court, capital defendants must demonstrate (1) good cause why the claim now being made was not included in the first filing, and (2) how the absence of that claim may have harmed the petitioner's ability to mount an effective defense.

C. Cruel and Unusual Punishments

The majority of justices on the U.S. Supreme Court today seem convinced of the constitutionality of the death penalty. Some justices continue, however, to view it as a barbarous punishment that has no place in civilized society. Also open to debate is the constitutionality of the methods for imposition of capital punishment. Questions concerning the use of hanging and the electric chair have troubled the Court in recent years.

The U.S. Supreme Court in *Roper* v. *Simmons,* decided March 1, 2005, held that the U.S. Constitution bars capital punishment for juvenile offenders who are younger than 18 years of age when they committed the crime.

VII. Intermediate Sanctions

Innovative sentencing options are known as intermediate sanctions. They are often imposed in lieu of more traditional sanctions. Intermediate sanctions include split sentencing, shock probation, shock incarceration, mixed-sentencing, community service, home confinement, and intensive supervision. A split sentence requires the offender to serve a brief period of confinement followed by a term of probation. Split sentences are frequently imposed on youthful offenders who commit minor crimes in hopes that the threat of further sanctions might deter the person from additional law violations. Shock probation is much like split sentencing in that the offender serves a relatively short period of confinement in correctional custody and is then released by the court. Shock incarceration makes use of boot camp type of correctional programs followed by probation.

Mixed sentencing requires offenders to perform some type of community service along with brief periods of time in confinement, which is often served as weekends in jail. Community service is a sentencing alternative which requires the offender to spend at least part of his or her time working for a public agency. Intensive probation is an alternative form of sentencing which includes probation, but imposes especially strict requirements upon the offenders. Home confinement, also called house arrest, requires that offenders be confined in their homes, and sometimes makes use of electronic monitoring to ensure that they do not leave during the hours of confinement. Intermediate sanctions are generally available with relatively unthreatening, non-violent, and first-time offenders.

CAPSTONE CASES: LEARNING ISSUES

Weeks v. *Angelone*

    1.   What was the issue in this case?

    2.   Why did the Court affirm the conviction?

PRACTICE TEST QUESTIONS

MULTIPLE CHOICE

_____ 14.1.   Which punishment goal is the most punishment oriented of all sentencing goals?
    a. general deterrence
    b. specific deterrence
    c. rehabilitation
    d. retribution

_____ 14.2.   Which punishment goal is directed toward preventing the individual sentenced to punishment from committing future offenses?
    a. general deterrence
    b. specific deterrence
    c. rehabilitation
    d. restoration

_____ 14.3.   Which punishment goal is designed to deter others from committing breaking the law?
    a. general deterrence
    b. specific deterrence
    c. restoration
    d. retribution

_____ 14.4.   Which punishment goal is designed to reform the criminal?
    a. incapacitation
    b. specific deterrence
    c. rehabilitation
    d. retribution

_____ 14.5.   Which sentencing goal attempts to restore victims to a state akin to that which they were in prior to victimization?
    a. incapacitation

b. specific deterrence

c. restoration

d. retribution

____ 14.6.   Which sentencing goal makes use of imprisonment to reduce the likelihood that an offender will be capable of committing future offenses?

a. incapacitation

b. specific deterrence

c. rehabilitation

d. retribution

____ 14.7.   California's three-strikes legislation reflects which sentencing goal?

a. incapacitation

b. specific deterrence

c. rehabilitation

d. retribution

____ 14.8.   What type of sentence does a defendant receive who is sentenced to serve a period of confinement as determined by the department of corrections?

a. concurrent

b. consecutive

c. determinate

d. indeterminate

____ 14.9.   What type of sentence is an individual serving who is awarded two six-year sentences and is scheduled for release from prison in twelve years?

a. concurrent

b. consecutive

c. determinate

d. indeterminate

____ 14.10.   What type of sentence is an individual serving who is scheduled to be released from prison in seven years after receiving two seven-year prison terms?

a. concurrent

b. consecutive

c. determinate

d. indeterminate

____ 14.11.   What type of sentence is an individual serving who receives a ten-year prison term?

a. concurrent

b. consecutive

c. determinate

d. indeterminate

_____ 14.12. Which sentencing principle refers to the belief that the severity of sanctions should bear a direct relationship to the seriousness of the crime committed?

a. proportionality

b. determinate

c. social debt

d. indeterminate

_____ 14.13. Which sentencing principle counts an offender's criminal history as an objectively recognized factor in any sentencing decision?

a. proportionality

b. equity

c. social debt

d. indeterminate

_____ 14.14. Which sentencing principle is based on a concern with social equality and contends that similar crimes should be punished with the same degree of severity, regardless of the social or personal characteristics of offenders?

a. proportionality

b. equity

c. social debt

d. indeterminate

_____ 14.15. The U.S. Supreme Court in the case of _____ upheld plea bargaining.

a. *Brady* v. *United States*

b. *Furman* v. *Georgia*

b. *Mistretta* v. *United States*

c. *Wilkerson* v. *Utah*

_____ 14.16. In 1972, the U.S. Supreme Court in the case of _____ invalidated Georgia's death penalty statute.

a. *Gregg* v. *Georgia*

b. *Furman* v. *Georgia*

b. *Mistretta* v. *United States*

c. *Wilkerson* v. *Utah*

_____ 14.17. In 1976, the U.S. Supreme Court in the case of _____ upheld Georgia's new death penalty statute.

a. *Gregg* v. *Georgia*

b. *Furman* v. *Georgia*

b. *McCleskey* v. *Zandt*

c. *Wilkerson* v. *Utah*

___ 14.18. In which case did the U.S. Supreme Court establish a two-prong test to limit the number of appeals that a condemned person may bring to the federal courts?

a. *Gregg* v. *Georgia*

b. *Furman* v. *Georgia*

b. *McCleskey* v. *Zandt*

c. *Wilkerson* v. *Utah*

___ 14.19. Which sentencing alternative requires the individual to spend at least part of his or her time working for a public agency?

a. home confinement

b. mixed sentencing

c. intensive supervision

d. community service

___ 14.20. Which sentencing alternative imposes especially strict requirements upon individuals on probation?

a. home confinement

b. mixed sentencing

c. intensive supervision

d. community service

TRUE/FALSE

___ 14.21 The need to assign blame and the need to punish wrongdoers may be fundamental human qualities.

___ 14.22. Today, the just deserts philosophy is not very popular.

___ 14.23. One purpose of retribution is to get back at the offender.

___ 14.24. General deterrence is intended to deter the individual sentenced to punishment from committing future offenses.

___ 14.25. Rehabilitation programs may also include a punishment component.

___ 14.26. Rehabilitation may also be considered as resocialization.

___ 14.27. Restoration is a sentencing goal that seeks to restore the victims to a state akin to that which they were in prior to victimization.

____ 14.28.   Incapacitation is a strategy that makes use of community service as the primary sentencing option.

____ 14.29.   Three-strikes legislation represents a philosophy of selective incapacitation.

____ 14.30.   In most jurisdictions, juries are the primary sentencing authorities.

KEY CONCEPTS

Identify the below key concepts from Chapter 14 of the text:

_____ 14.1.   The most punishment-oriented of all sentencing goals.

_____ 14.2.   Model of criminal sentencing that holds that criminal offenders deserve the punishment they receive at the hands of the state.

_____ 14.3.   An attempt to reform a criminal offender.

_____ 14.4.   Goal of criminal sentencing that seeks to prevent others from committing crimes.

_____ 14.5.   Goal of sentencing that seeks to prevent a particular offender from engaging in repeat criminality.

_____ 14.6.   Sentencing goal that seeks to make victims and the community "whole again."

_____ 14.7.   Use of imprisonment to reduce the likelihood that an offender will be capable ot committing future offenses.

_____ 14.8.   Sentencing goal that builds on restitution and community participation in an attempt to make the victim "whole again."

_____ 14.9.   Sentencing principle that holds that the severity of sanctions should bear a direct relationship to the seriousness of the crime.

____ 14-10.   Fixed sentences.

FACTUAL SCENARIOS

1.   Joseph's father is dying of cancer. The father, who is suffering a lot of pain, requests Joseph to kill him. Joseph does and is convicted of murder. The judge is trying to determine the appropriate sentence to impose in this case from a permissible range of 15 years to life. If the judge believes that the goal of punishment should be deterrence, what factors should he consider?

2.   Ted, an 18-year-old, is convicted of robbery. It is his first adult offense. He has a juvenile record. He is married with a two-year-old child. During the robbery, he used a gun. No one was hurt in the robbery. What sentence should he receive? Give reasons for your choice.

CROSSWORD 14

Across

5. Principle based on social concerns.

6. ____ corpus

7. Use of confinement to prevent the individual from committing other crimes.

8. Seeks to make victim and community whole again.

9. Convicted criminals are ordered to pay ____ .

Down

1. Suspended sentence

2. ___ in sentencing.

3. Act of taking revenge on a criminal perpetrator

4. An attempt to reform a criminal.